FIRED AT FIFTY

FIRED AT FIFTY

Stop Looking For Work
And Discover What You
Were Meant To Do

Christine Till

First Published in Canada 2013 by Influence Publishing

Cover design and layout: Greg Salisbury
Author photo: Carlos Taylhardat - Carlos@artofheadshots.com

DISCLAIMER: This is a work of non-fiction. The information is of a general nature to help you on the subject of business. Readers of this publication agree that neither Christine Till, nor her publisher will be held responsible or liable for damages that may be alleged or resulting directly or indirectly from their use of this publication. All external links are provided as a resource only and are not guaranteed to remain active for any length of time. Neither the publisher nor the author can be held accountable for the information provided by, or actions resulting from accessing these resources.

For Rodger
Who supported me and my dream in more ways than one.

For Julie
Who spent many hours helping me with the editing
and publishing of this book.

Thank you both for believing in me.

Acknowledgements

I truly believe that people come into our lives at certain times for a reason. As I have watched my book unfold and the events in my life leading up to it, I realize that Fired at Fifty would never have become a reality if it were not for these special people in my life.

When I decided to write my book I thought I knew what I was doing and now I am so pleased that I met Julie Salisbury, my publisher with Influence Publishing. She demonstrated to me the importance of having a publisher. I would never have come this far without her. I feel that because of Julie I now have a marketable product and a platform for my business that will help many people who are fired at fifty.

Many thanks to all my contributors. You have selflessly shared some of your most personal thoughts and experiences. Your submissions have helped make my book what it is today. I love your stories! I know that my readers will enjoy them too.

Thank you to all the wonderful people who were my guests on my podcast show. Each and every one of you has had an impact on my life in some way. I feel like each of you has been my own personal coach while we were together chatting over Skype about your business and why you do what you do, and how you do what you do. You probably did not realize at the time how much of an impact you have been in my life. You have all helped me to see that I could be so much better than I thought I could be. You inspired me to reach to new heights and stretch beyond what I could ever have dreamed.

Janet Love Morrison, my Editor, taught me that there is a process to everything, even writing a book.

There are so many people who have shown me their love and how much they care for me, especially in these last two years. They have helped me have the confidence and belief in myself that I needed to complete my dream of becoming a published author. Sometimes I have to pinch myself to realize that this is not a "pipe dream." This is real and all these people really do care about me. I want them to know that I care about them too.

It is my sincere desire that the words I have shared with you, my reader, in Fired at Fifty will inspire you to not only help yourself "find out what you were meant to do" and also "find out who you were meant to be."

Love & Blessings,
Christine E. Till
The Marketing Mentress

Table of Contents

Epigraph

"When you do the things that most people won't do, when you don't feel like doing them, you will have the things that most people won't have."
Unknown

Before success comes in any man's life, he's sure to meet with much temporary defeat and, perhaps some failures. When defeat overtakes a man, the easiest and the most logical thing to do is to quit. That's exactly what the majority of men do.
Napoleon Hill

Feeling sorry for yourself, and your present condition, is not only a waste of energy but the worst habit you could possibly have.
Dale Carnegie

Chapter One

Failure

On January 4, 2011, I walked into my office looking forward to a new year of sales and marketing cheerfully greeting everyone with my usual, "Happy Wednesday!" wondering why everyone was a little reserved. It was as though everyone knew something I didn't know.

Then my boss invited me to step into the boardroom - I didn't even have my coat off yet. In the boardroom my boss informed me that I was the hardest working person he had ever known and he had kept me on because of my work ethic. Little did he know that I was burning out trying to build up his company. He said my services weren't needed any longer. Sales hadn't improved significantly over the past two years and he had hit his bottom line. As I sat and listened, I remembered I was the eighth in a long line of sales people who had previously worked for his company. It seemed when sales didn't improve within six to eight months: they were let go and a new sales person was hired.

In the time I spent working for him I recognized the fact that there was a lot of money invested in training all these people: one only has to do the math. Didn't he know the best salesperson in the company should be him - the owner? A good boss should be the one who delegates sales. If he is his own best salesman, he could train his staff the way he believes is necessary for success. But that was that - I was fired and asked to clear out my desk.

People call it being pink slipped, or laid off, or downsized; but quite frankly, it's just fired. He softened the blow by handing me

1

a two-week severance check. Phew! At least I didn't have to go back to work with everyone knowing I was fired.

I couldn't get my things packed up and out of that office fast enough. I felt as though no one liked me or wanted me around. The staff members who I thought were my friends were suddenly a little on the cool side - you get my drift. Actually, I feel they just didn't know how to handle the situation. It was uncomfortable for everyone. Oh sure, I put on a good stiff upper lip as I continued to be fairly cheerful, but not overly so. I just got to work clearing out my desk. It wasn't just my office cubicle that had to be cleared out though; there was also the company car. You know how things can accumulate in the nooks and crannies in a car. Well, it took me around an hour to zoom through both. Once I was done, one of the other staff members drove me home so they could bring the company car back.

How humiliating. One minute I was driving this cute little car with a three quarter wrap and then I was a passenger in it. I felt like an old lady. I arrived home and shed many tears. Here I was, jobless in the latter half of my life having worked my fingers to the bone for every employer I've had. However, this wasn't the first time I was fired. Therefore, I thought I could just snap back, get back to work and be on top of the world again in no time.

Have you ever been fired from a job? It doesn't feel so great, does it? Do you know what? In the shock I suddenly remembered every humiliating experience I had ever had in my life. I mulled over each experience again and again wondering how I could have done things differently and I asked myself, was it truly my fault? I remembered how I was treated at every job. Were there similarities? Could I have done things differently? Was it me? Or was I just the brunt of a much bigger problem? I wondered, what is wrong with me? Why can't I just stay at a job longer than a few years? Sometimes it was only a few months before I was pink-slipped again. Was I so unemployable that I couldn't fit into any position I ever entered? My whole world collapsed around my head and I felt utterly alone, unwanted, and unneeded. What was I to do now?

I sat and pondered … here I was; fifty years old. I let myself pine for a short time, but while the tears were still fresh I resolved the situation in my mind: I will never give up. I even said it aloud. Whatever I have to do, whatever it takes, I will always stay strong. I was determined to gain control over my emotions and tears. It probably wasn't the best idea, but it worked to keep me strong.

There I was: without a plan, without any preparation, and without an income. Where was I to go from here? I wasn't ready for this. I found myself five to ten years short of the financial goals I had set for my retirement. How was I going to survive? What was I going to do? Needless to say, I was lost.

History repeating itself

I have wondered why I have such a love for people, even after being treated poorly over the years. When I was in grade three the kids at school started calling me "the witch". In those days the community nurse came twice a year to measure and weigh all the children in school. I was always the tallest and the heaviest in the class. After the nurse gathered her data she would then give the required immunizations. She would call out everyone's height and weight to the person who was writing down the records for her. Everything was done alphabetically, starting with "A". My last name started with an "S", so I had the chance to sit and listen to all the heights and weights of almost the entire class. Then it was my turn. The nurse called out my height and there was an audible sigh throughout the classroom - I was 15 pounds heavier and head and shoulders taller than everyone in the class. Someone called out, "She's a witch!" and that name stuck with me throughout school.

I didn't have any friends in school and I wasn't ever invited to any parties. So, in grade eleven I decided to have a party at my house and invited everyone in my class to attend. My mom worked hard baking, and she made all her specialties including Sloppy Joes. My mom made the best Sloppy Joes in the country. Well, the day of my party arrived and nobody showed up. I waited for half an hour and still nobody arrived. Then, one of the guys came to tell me that nobody was coming to my party. I was stunned, even though I had already surmised as much. He invited me to go to the movies with him, so we went to watch a show in the local movie theatre. He was a kind soul.

Years later in 1977, I was 28 years old with three small children. I was a full-time mother and ran my own ranch near Red Deer, Alberta. I spent many evenings canning food, sewing jeans, and making sheepskin coats for my children. I was overloaded. I felt I was going to have a nervous breakdown. When I was in town one day I met a girlfriend of mine. When she saw me, she asked if I was okay. I told her exactly how I felt.

She stopped me right there and said she had something important to share with me. Her husband was a sociologist and he counselled people on social services assistance in the province of Alberta. He said virtually every time a person has a nervous breakdown, or a mental breakdown; they have made the decision to give up. Then, she proceeded to tell me that once a person has a nervous breakdown they are never the same again and they can never regain the full strength of their mind and character. If anything, once someone has had one nervous breakdown, they're prone to having another one and another one. Once they have given up the first time; they generally end up on medication for the rest of their lives. The medication dulls their spirits and keeps them from functioning to their full potential. She proceeded to list the symptoms of a nervous breakdown and one of these symptoms was crying uncontrollably without being able to stop.

Let me tell you, I felt like crying all the time and quite often I had tears running down my face. How could she tell? I must have looked pretty bad. Well, right then and there I decided that what ever happened in my life I wasn't ever going to give up. I didn't want to be less than I was (whatever that was) and I definitely didn't want to be on some kind of medication for the rest of my life.

Kicking and Screaming into the Twenty First Century

That life experience served me well, it gave me the courage to meet my challenges and rise. Now, let's move along to the mid-eighties when I was faced with a challenge of another kind: I was forced to learn how to use a computer.

My boss (at that time) told me he was going to get rid of my beloved IBM Selectric typewriter and he would be replacing it with an Apple 2E. I was shocked. He advised me to get some computer training - and fast because he was making the change soon. I thought he would never get rid of his IBM Selectric, even if he did get a computer. I thought people would always need a typewriter, no matter what new fangled gismo was invented. Boy, was I wrong. I walked into my office one fine morning and sitting in the middle of my desk was an Apple 2E computer. Imagine that? The day before he didn't even tell me that I was going to be in another world of typing the following day. The nerve. Well, I searched all over for my beloved IBM Selectric and it wasn't anywhere to be found. Can you believe it? There I was with this miniature monster sitting smack in the middle of my desk: and I knew nothing about it. How could my boss do this to me? Then it dawned on me. He had warned me several months ago that this was going to happen, but I never believed him.

That evening I brought my ten-year-old son into the office just to show me how to turn the flaming thing on. Well, my son showed me a few other things too. At least I could look like I knew what I was doing when my boss saw me the next morning.

That life experience was an introduction to the next tsunami of technology that was coming my way. It was invisible to my naked eye, but it kept surging forward year by year, month by month, day by day, and minute by minute. It started with email. It kept swelling into on-line searching, and then to the new on-line media. Life as I knew it wouldn't ever be the same. I found myself completely consumed by this tsunami of technology. Maybe I couldn't see it, but I felt its presence everywhere: social media had arrived.

Time went on, the years passed as I was working and raising my family. Then, in 2008 I started working for Mr. No in the senior health care industry. I worked as the Director of Sales and Marketing for a senior homecare company from June 2008 until the end of December 2010.

Their business philosophy was to have me make cold calls every day; to meet people for coffee; and to give presentations on different senior related topics. I gave these presentations wherever I could book the time at senior activity centres. However, research (done world wide from their head office) showed that 73% of seniors make their decisions with their adult children. Well, where were they during the day when I was doing a presentation at a senior centre? They were at work. Then, in the evenings they were sitting in front of their computers with tears streaming down their cheeks trying to find a way to ease their pain of being sandwiched between aging parents, their own families, and careers.

It just so happened that I was speaking with my eldest son around that same time. He was helping me with creating an on-line marketing plan for Mr. No's company. He was (and still is) a wizard with technology and had used podcasting to find himself a job. He had used LinkedIn to find business people who were associated with the kinds of companies he wanted to work for. After he found them, he would invite them to be a guest on his show. They would always be intrigued and flattered that he had picked them. Before and after the interview there was always an opportunity for him to chat with his guests and they would ask him what he did for a living. He would tell them what he was looking for and they would give him referrals. It worked like a charm. He ended up with several job interviews and eventually landed a good job: all as a result of his podcasting initiative.

From his life experience he offered to help me in my efforts with Mr. No's company and we decided to create a podcasting show for me. He set me up with podcasting and soon I was interviewing people on my show called, "Eldercare 911". My intent was to show myself as an eldercare specialist and I started my podcast show to reach out on-line to the baby boomers. Here was my son, once again, teaching me about technology and that's how I got my start with my podcasting career in 2009.

Lucky for me I have become quite proficient with using social media. Funny, it all started with me having to prove to Mr. No that he needed to use social media to market his business. Well, I never succeeded in convincing him to pay for my time spent with social media, but I sure acquired a huge education.

Social media swept (and continues to sweep) the world. I found myself being sucked in with invitations to join different sites such as Facebook, Twitter, YouTube, LinkedIn, Foursquare, Viadeo, Hootsuite, and SproutSocial - just to name a few. There were so many platforms and it was a challenge to know which ones were the best to get involved with, or even take the time to learn.

I spent hours upon hours and days upon days studying, reading, and learning about the Internet and the different platforms of social media. I found I could spend 24/7 just sitting at my computer working on my social media platforms, researching, and learning all about the Internet platforms for communication and study, but time was of the essence here. I simply didn't have enough time to let this tsunami consume me. I had to choose the platforms I felt suited my needs the best, because by now I had combined my traditional marketing with on-line platforms.

I spent many hours in the evenings and on weekends recording and publishing my podcast shows and posting them throughout my social media. Do you know what? The very first time I posted one of my podcasts on Facebook I had a response within an hour from a gal who said, "Oh my gosh! I had no idea something like this was available! I sure could have used this service when my 95-year-old dad was alive!"

For me it was a natural transition from sales and marketing in the traditional sense to using the on-line platforms. I had been using these same platforms to get clients for the senior care company. Now, I could use them to garner my own clients.

So, here I was in 2011 (two years later) and Mr. No had just fired me. After recovering from the shock my husband and I got involved with a network marketing company that offered discounts on technology services such as: video phones, cell phones, high speed internet, internet sticks, local and long distance, cable TV services, and a host of other services.

It caught us at a time of desperation in our lives and we jumped on the bandwagon believing this was going to be our answer to all our financial challenges. Oh-oh, think again. Three months later, two thousand dollars invested, friends lost in the process and we were deeper into our credit cards and unable to sponsor even one person into the business. We couldn't keep spending money without making any. We had to stop building the business. We were back at square one again. Only our square one was a minus square one, we were in debt.

It takes a special personality type to build a network marketing business. You need to look for the centres of influence that will become your top twenty percent who will build eighty percent of your business. It takes time and money to build a big network marketing business, and that is what most people don't realize. We just didn't have the money to carry on. If my readers are considering a networking business as a quick fix, I hope they will learn from our life experience.

I was soon back chatting with my son. He believed I could use the same podcasting method he used to find a job. I thought this was a brilliant idea. He suggested I could become a "marketing mentor," because marketing had been my life for over 20 years. Marketing Mentor? That sounded awfully masculine to me. I wanted something more feminine. He then suggested, "The Marketing Mentress!". My show could be "The Marketing Mentress Show". My next question was whom would I invite to be guests? Thus, I began a quest for great material.

I decided to start with LinkedIn. It was here I came in contact with a lovely woman in the financial planning business whom specializes in women's finances. Check out my website to see who that was at www.practicalpodcasting.com. "The Marketing Mentress Show" débuted on January 21, 2011. After that pilot episode, it was through LinkedIn that I was able to continue finding key people to interview. We would chat about their business and what type of marketing they found worked best for them. It was a blast! I loved every person I interviewed and felt I would hire them myself, or purchase their products and books. And not only did I target people who I thought would be great on my show, but also those who I wanted to trade services with.

Thinking back to that fateful day in January 2011, and the year leading up to it, I remember feeling baffled why all my hard work learning wasn't paying off - especially with all the social media I was creating. I see now that I was on to something great. I just needed more time to create exposure for them. It's a lesson I learned the hard way. It takes time to get established on-line. It takes time and patience to build up your reputation and presence: you can't expect instant results as my old boss had expected.

I threw myself into my work. I was working 12 to 16 hours a day non-stop. I was reading, sending emails, looking for work, learning more about social media, perfecting my on-line skills, and doing podcast interviews. Most of the authors I interviewed would send me a copy of their book, so I could read it before our interview. As a result, my library has grown immensely. It has given me more insight on how I would shape my business and reach out to find people who needed and wanted my services.

As I interviewed people on my show, I discovered that each and every person became my own personal coach in some way. I learned something I could implement either into my own personal growth or my business.

Everyone was invited to be my guest for free. All they had to do was show up and answer my questions. They all loved being on my show. I made them sound like a million bucks and they loved the limelight. Do you know what I found from this experience? I discovered that people want to reciprocate. Many of my guests were so pleased with being on my show that they wanted to give back. As a result, I received countless recommendations from them, marketing ideas, coaching, financial advice, and many other words of wisdom.

The people I interviewed would offer to help me in some way or offer a trade. They complimented me about my level of professionalism, how much they enjoyed the interview, and how I made them feel so comfortable. All their words of affirmation were music to my ears. Little did I realize that my podcast guests were secretly building up my feelings of self-worth: and this really helped my self-esteem. Through these wonderful individuals, I began to feel brave enough to stand in front of people at networking meetings. They helped me to find my voice and ask for what I needed.

When I suddenly found myself out of work that fateful day in 2011, it was quite a shock. It brought up a whole myriad of emotions that I hadn't realized I had. There were feelings of no self-worth, being used, being unwanted, being a failure, rejection, being stupid, and worthless. Quite frankly, I felt like running away and disappearing and never contacting anyone: not even my family or my husband. I just wanted to disappear and never be seen again. I just wanted to roam the land until I was dead and gone. I felt like I had failed everyone and everything in my life. Today I feel so different. People are wonderful. Offering people the gift of a podcast will always be part of who I am and what I do.

Throughout 2011 I applied for jobs (what few jobs were available in my field) I was qualified for, but I didn't ever hear back from them. Now, I'm not a frump without any energy. I present myself very professionally and sometimes, well, quite frankly, I think I have more energy in my little finger than a whole room full of 20-year-olds.

I had very few job interviews. Four to be exact; however, I was finally offered a job at $10 an hour. Do you know the feeling when you can't move a muscle and you just sit there in stunned silence? I went out to my car and sat there in the parking lot thinking, do I take this job and work like this for the rest of my life, never reaching my financial goals for retirement and never being able to relax and take life a little easier? Not that I ever would lay around just eating bon-bons. Or do I stay on Employment Insurance (EI) and keep looking?

As the tears streamed down my cheeks, suddenly I felt awash with all the failures in my life once again. I was a failure, plain and simple. I wasn't any good to anyone. I hated myself. I was too fat. I ate too much. I needed more exercise. I thought I could never work for anyone ever again. I'm a misfit. Nobody likes me. Everybody hates me. You know the drill.

I knew that if I took the job, I would be scraping by and be exhausted at the end of the day without the energy to work on my dreams and goals. But EI would only last a few months and then what was I going to do? I had only until the middle of July 2011 before my EI benefits were going to be cut off. I had to work fast. Time was precious. Well, I decided to stay on EI and keep looking while working on my dreams and goals.

It had occurred to me that I may not find work again, so what was I going to do in the meantime? What did I have to offer that would be of value to other people and bring in an income at the same time? I have read many books and taken many courses. The common denominator in all of them stated to sit down and make a list of all your strengths and weaknesses: right now on my piece of paper all I could see were my weaknesses.

I tell you all of this because it was through my deepest struggles of self-worth that I found my value and my mission. I know now what I'm meant to do. I'm to help other people who are going through the exact same challenges. It's my belief that I can help them: just as my son helped me.

On my journey I have met many people who were also fired at fifty and faced the same challenges as me. Many of these people have been guests on my show and whether they knew it or not, they had a significant role in my evolution as The Marketing Mentress. Each person has touched my heart and mind. They have inspired me in establishing myself in my business and in finding what I was meant to do. I asked them to contribute to my book so my readers can benefit from their advice and experience too.

I would like to end this chapter first with a contribution from Doug Dickerson and finish with one from Richard G. Earl.

Doug Dickerson was introduced to me through Phil Taylor's LinkedIn group. They both have groups on LinkedIn. Since Doug and I have met we have had several Skype exchanges and discussions on different aspects of marketing, specifically the senior care industry. He has written a book and I believe is in the process of publishing his second one. We hit it off great from the first time we chatted over Skype. He resides near Charleston, South Carolina. Doug is also involved in the senior care industry and we have chatted on several occasions exchanging ideas to help him and his organization.

I invited author and professional speaker, Doug Dickerson, to share a few words with us. Thank you Doug.

"The Path of Your Second Half"
by Doug Dickerson

*The real test of a man is not when he plays the role that he
wants for himself, but when he plays the role destiny has for
him.*

Vaclav Havel

In 2009, during the dark hours of the world's financial
crisis, it wasn't a great time to be in a job transition.
Just like millions of others caught up in an economic
tsunami I was in a transition not of my choosing. As
frightening as it was, it was also a time to recapture
simmering passions and lay claim to a new destiny.
The truth is: life happens. Bad things happen to
good people and the best-laid plans don't always
turn out as we had hoped. At that time, life was at an
intermission. Soon the curtains would be raised on the
second half. Did I mention that it was a frightening
time?

In his acclaimed book, "Halftime: Changing Your
Game Plan from Success to Significance," Bob Buford
offers powerful insights for those facing the beginning
of the second half.

Buford writes, "The game is won or lost in the
second half, not the first half. It's possible to make
some mistakes in the first half and still have time to
recover, but it's harder to do that in the second half.
In the second half you should, at long last, know what
you have to work with. And you know the playing field,
the world you live in. You have experienced enough
victory to know how hard the game is most of the
time, and yet how easy it seems when the conditions
are just right. You have experienced enough pain and
disappointment to know that while losing a few rounds
is certainly no fun, loss is survivable and sometimes
uncovers the best that is in you."

As you face the advent on the second half I have good news for you - the experiences of your first half have uniquely positioned you for a strong second half. Allow me to share with you what I refer to as the "5 R's" for a great second half. Take these simple principles to heart as you chart your course with the belief that your second half will far exceed your first.

Regain your confidence. Whatever the cause or circumstances surrounding your transition it's important not to allow it to cause a setback in your confidence. While it's easy to sit back and sulk about mistakes made or to assign blame, the bottom line is without confidence it will be hard to move forward.

The American painter, John Sargent once painted a panel of roses. He was highly praised by his critics. It was a small picture, but it approached perfection. Although Sargent was offered a high price for it on many occasions, he refused to sell. He considered it his best work and was very proud. Whenever he was deeply discouraged and doubtful of his abilities as an artist, he would look at it and remind himself, "I painted that." Then his confidence and ability would come back to him.

Being in transition isn't fun and the temptation to be discouraged is an ever-present reality. But notice what Sargent did to overcome doubts related to his abilities as an artist: He would look at his most prized work and remind himself of what he did. You must do the same. Stop looking at your mistakes, or what you should have done, look at what you did right.

Regaining your confidence begins when you remind yourself that your God-given talents and abilities haven't been bestowed in vain and that there is a place for you to invest them. Don't think in terms of what you have lost or how bad you have it, but dare to look at how far you can go with your gifts and what a wonderful contributor you will be in your next assignment.

Renew your goals. Now that you find yourself in transition it is time to renew your goals. The landscape ahead of you looks much different than the scenery behind you. You will need to reset the compass and chart the course wisely.

I read a story of a ship's captain who looked into the dark night and saw faint lights in the distance. He immediately told his signalman to send a message, "Alter your course ten degrees south." Promptly a return message was received, "Alter your course ten degrees north."

The captain was angered: his command had been ignored. He sent a second message, "Alter your course ten degrees south. I am the captain!" Soon another message was received, "Alter your course ten degrees north. I'm seaman third class Jones." The captain sent a third message, knowing the fear it would evoke, "Alter your course ten degrees south. I am a battleship." Then the reply came, "Alter your course ten degrees north. I'm a lighthouse."

Like the captain, you may be unwillingly on your present course and it can be stressful. You're on a new course and you're not happy about it, but if you want to safely navigate your way forward you must be flexible and willing to take advice and change course.

Renewing your goals is simply drawing up new blueprints to take you where you want to go. Your desired goals and outcomes may not have changed, but how you reach them will have. What new skills do you need? Do you need to go back to school? Who can help you? What short-term actions do you need to take? These and other questions must be answered. Make your plan and chart the course. As you renew your goals you can renew your passions. Ignite them.

Reject the negative. For many, times are still tough. Negative news and attitudes can wear you down. However, it's the negative thoughts you entertain which can cause the most damage. I know from my own experience that those were the hardest to overcome. It's essential to fill your mind with positive thoughts.

In Reader's Digest, a few years back, Steve Goodier shared a story about hummingbirds and vultures that both fly over the deserts in the United States. All the vultures see is rotting meat, because that is what they look for. Vultures thrive on that diet. On the other hand, hummingbirds ignore the smelly flesh of dead animals. Instead, they look for the colorful blossoms of desert plants. Vultures live in what was. They live on the past. They fill themselves with what is dead and gone. Hummingbirds live on what is. They seek new life. They fill themselves with freshness and life. Each bird finds what it is looking for. The analogy is: we all do.

As you walk through your transition keep your thoughts and attitudes positive. You may not have chosen the road you are now on, but where this road takes you is in large part determined by your ability to reject negative thoughts and focus on positive ones.

Refuse to give up. In his book "Hand Me Another Brick" Charles Swindoll tells the story of Thomas Edison and the challenge he faced after fire destroyed his warehouse where many of his inventions and work were stored.

As a fire tore through the film room, within minutes all the packing compounds, celluloid for records and film, and other flammable goods were in flames. Fire companies from eight surrounding towns arrived, but the heat was so intense and the water pressure so low that attempting to douse the flames was futile.

Everything was destroyed. Edison was 67 years old. The damages to his building exceeded two million dollars, but he was only insured for $238,000 because it was made of concrete and thought to be fireproof. Would his spirit be broken?

During the fire, Edison's son Charles searched frantically for his father. He finally found him; he was calmly watching the fire. "My heart ached for him," said Charles. "He was 67, no longer a young man, and everything was going up in flames. When he saw me, he shouted, 'Charles, where is your mother?' When I told him I didn't know, he said, 'Find her. Bring her here. She will never see anything like this as long as she lives.'"

The next morning Edison looked at the ruins and said, "There is great value in disaster. All our mistakes are burned up. Thank God we can start anew." Three weeks after the fire Edison managed to deliver the first phonograph.

I don't know what you see when you look at the rubble of your disappointment or if you doubt you can ever recover, but like Edison, let me encourage you to believe that your best days are not behind you, they are before you. When you choose to work through the fire and not give up, you position yourself for great possibilities. Refuse to give up.

Re-enter with purpose. Making the most of the second half of your life is about living your life with a renewed purpose. In as much as you didn't choose to be in your transition, the purpose by which you emerge from it can make a world of difference.

In his book, "Up, Down, or Sideways", my friend Mark Sanborn writes, "If you think of value as an equation, it would look like this: $V = E + E + SE$, or Value equals Expectations plus Education plus Something Extra. The question facing most of us (and our organizations) is: What's our something extra?

As you emerge from your transition with confidence, you can make new goals and add value to others. Reject the negative and refuse to give up. In doing so, you can live your life with purpose and destiny.

A life of purpose doesn't know any age barriers and

through this season of your life you are being prepared for a greater degree of contribution. The second half of your life awaits you; enter it with all the confidence and satisfaction of knowing that the game isn't won or lost in the first half of life. As you start the second half, the ball is in your court, the odds are in your favor, and a bright future awaits you.

Doug Dickerson
My Blog:
www.dougsmanagementmoment.blogspot.com
Follow me on Twitter:
www.twitter.com/managemntmoment
My radio show:
www.blogtalkradio.com/managementmoment
International Business Times contributor page:
www.ibtimes.com/user/9513

I met Richard G. Earl on LinkedIn. Shortly after, he was my guest on The Marketing Mentress Show. As we got to know each other, he started to teach me about social media and how to use auto-responders for I had mentioned to him that I was spending inordinate amounts of time with each of my social media trying to keep posts up and didn't have time for anything else. Richard opened my eyes to a whole new world of social media planning and preparation through the use of auto-responders. (For those of you who do not know what a social media auto-responder is, it is a platform that you can schedule your messages to go out through your Twitter, Facebook, LinkedIn, etc. You can schedule these messages to be posted as many times as you want on any date you choose and at any time you choose. Then, you don't have to worry about being on them for more than a few minutes a day just to respond to people that respond to your posted messages. How cool is that?!)

Beached! The Beginning not the End!

When Christine invited me to offer a contribution to her upcoming book "Fired at Fifty", the first thought was what do I know about this? But reflecting on the last seven decades, common elements have emerged which could be useful to contribute.

I decided the best way to do this seemed through sharing some of my life experiences, and some of those of others. These all centre on a lifestyle and philosophy of self-responsibility, sufficiency, reliance, and determination.

For me this philosophy stemmed from being born into a world at war in Hassocks (www.owl.li/d7SXe) on the south coast of England. At that time very little of anything was available. Rationing played a huge part of daily life; there really was no other choice but to get on with it. Self-sufficiency in all aspects of life was very much the name of the game. To hunt, fish, trap, glean whatever there was from the garden was very much second nature. What wasn't available was either not missed or was traded.

We all experience degrees of traumatic life events, "No", "Can't" and "Unemployable" are just some words not welcomed: at any age. To be written off by experts is always traumatic, but three times (in my case) defies logic, but not spirit.

In 1968 I was diagnosed with cancer and according to medical judgments my life expectancy wasn't promising. At one particularly low point in the 1968 treatments, a really great guy, Sussex cancer expert Dr. Jan deWinter said to me one morning: "Live every day as if it was your last and then some day you'll be right." Not original, but it stuck with me over all the years.

(The quote is attributed to H.H. "Breaker" Morant see www.owl.li/d7Owh Australian folk hero? Plus many others, see Carpe Diem Quotes, Seize the Day

Sayings, Life is Short Quotations www.owl.li/d7ILt)

It's now over forty-four years since the first diagnosis of my terminal illness without any prognosis of survival. In the mid 1980s, I met with Dr. deWinter just to say thank you and meet some of his old team still with him.

The following years of my life saw a number of life transitions including moving to British Columbia, Canada, in 2002.

The following are some examples of other past and present figures that have demonstrated the living of self-responsibility, reliance, and determination.

Group Captain Sir Douglas Bader DSO & Bar, DFC & Bar was a Royal Air Force (RAF) fighter ace during the Second World War. He was credited with 20 aerial victories; four shared victories; six probables; one shared probable; and 11 enemy aircraft damaged.

Bader joined the RAF in 1928 and was commissioned in 1930. In December 1931, while attempting some aerobatics, he crashed and lost both his legs. Having been on the brink of death: he recovered. Bader retook his flight training, passed his check flights, and then requested reactivation as a pilot. Although there weren't any regulations applicable to his situation, he was retired on medical grounds.

After the outbreak of the Second World War in 1939, Bader returned to the RAF and was accepted as a pilot. He scored his first victories over Dunkirk during the Battle of France in 1940. He then took part in the Battle of Britain.

In August 1941 Bader was shot down and forced to evacuate his aircraft over German-occupied France and was captured. Despite his disability, Bader made a number of escape attempts and was eventually sent to the prisoner of war (POW) camp at Colditz Castle. At one point his artificial legs (replacements for the ones that were lost when he was shot down) were taken away to prevent further escape attempts.

Bader remained there until the First United States Army liberated the camp in April 1945.

Horatio Nelson, 1st Viscount Nelson, 1st Duke of Bronté, KB, was noted for his inspirational leadership and superb grasp of strategy and unconventional tactics. He was wounded several times in combat, losing one arm and the sight in one eye. Of his several victories, the best known and most notable was the Battle of Trafalgar in 1805 during which he was shot and killed. "Victory" his flagship is preserved and still a commissioned Royal Navy ship. The Battle of Trafalgar secured his position as one of Britain's most heroic figures. Numerous monuments including Nelson's Column in Trafalgar Square, London, commemorate him. A lesser-known fact is that he was very ill every time he put to sea.

Most recently… Oscar Pistorius of South Africa did what many thought was impossible. The 25-year-old sprinter nicknamed, "Blade Runner," became the first double amputee to compete in the London 2012 Summer Olympic Games.

Pistorius uses carbon-fiber artificial limbs to run with his double below-knee amputation, and participated in the 400-meter and 4 x 400-meter sprints. His participation in the Olympics represents a new chapter in sports history and proof that even disabilities can't hinder a determined and inspired athlete.

I guess all of the above heard "No", "Unemployable" and "Can't" a few times. Just pause and think for a moment about running on carbon-fiber artificial limbs, never mind competing in Olympic events.

Always keep in mind:

"The impossible can be done immediately, miracles take a little longer." The motto of the Canadian Engineers the First World War.

Talia Joy Castellano has been battling cancer for five years and just recently found out that pre-leukemia has now invaded her body.

There are a few treatment options left for Talia. If she decides to forgo treatment, doctors believe she will only have from four months to a year to live.

It's an incredibly sad story, but Talia has maintained an upbeat spirit while sharing her journey to the world online with her YouTube videos. She has over 100,000 subscribers on her YouTube channel who tune in to see how she's doing and check out her amazing make-up tutorials. This young girl, whose life has only just begun, blows any and all negatives out of the water.

Conclusion:
My story pales into insignificance if compared to those above. However, the philosophies of self-responsibility, sufficiency, reliance and determination, do not. They can apply to anything and everything.

> *"Chart your course. Our destiny is shaped by our thoughts and our actions. We cannot direct the wind, but we can adjust the sails."*
> Author unknown

Thanks for the opportunity to share.
Richard G Earl

Richard G Earl - HBG News on Current Affairs, Business & Promotions
www.richardearl.tel
Acknowledgements:
Wikipedia (Various)
YouTube (Various)
Dumb Little Man

Chapter Two

The Evolution of my Podcast Shows

At first I thought I could actually get paid for my podcasting services. However, after a year of inviting guests, marketing myself, and attending networking meetings I discovered there wasn't anyone who paid for podcast interviews. Many traded their coaching services, but I wasn't going to monetize my time this way.

From my experience, I suggest as you're trying to discover your skills, it's important that you observe how your services are being received. Then, that information will give clues about how you could make a living selling those skills.

In the following example (my experience of starting out with podcast interviews) you will see how I learned to identify who my customers really were.

One tactic I implemented while working with Mr. No was to go to different senior activity centres and retirement communities to give presentations on multiple topics. I spoke about the importance of initiating important conversations between seniors and their adult children while everyone was still healthy. For example, topics on personal health, finances, wills, powers of attorney, moving, and others. I would invite other presenters to join me such as a lawyer to speak about having a will drawn up and the importance of having a power of attorney. The sessions would vary, at times I would have someone from the senior living community speak with me or sometimes three or four of us would put on an information session.

However, I soon recognized that seniors wanted the

Fired at Fifty

information, but they didn't want to spend money on getting
outside help. The reasons for this were many, but primarily they
just didn't have the money. Over 80% of seniors can't afford to
pay for home care services. (As of 2005, in the province of BC
less than 5% of single women over 65 and just over 11% of
single men over age 65 had incomes over $60,000 and therefore
could afford a private-pay facility. www.cupe.ca/updir/CUPE-
long-term-care-seniors-care-summary.pdf)

They didn't want to spend their money - even if they had it.
They didn't know how long they would live and they wanted
to leave something for their children, not that all their children
wanted or needed their money.

They were afraid of losing their independence. Seniors felt if
they accepted help, they would then lose control of their lives.
They didn't want someone else to tell them where to go and how
to do it.

They were afraid of becoming even frailer if they had someone
else doing their daily chores for them. They believed if they
stopped pushing the vacuum; lugging around heavy cleaning
tools; and cleaning their own yards that they would deteriorate
more quickly, physically, and mentally.

Now, I mentioned in my first chapter that children of seniors
were working during the day while I would be giving my
presentations. People's lives are busy, that's just a fact. I used to
teach beginner piano lessons and I recall a forty-five year old
mom who would bring her two children for lessons, drop them
off, and run to cook dinner for her parents. Then, she would
dash back, pick up her children and they would eat take-out food
in the car as they went off to their soccer practice. This Mom
would drop off her children at the soccer field and run off again
to help her parents get ready for bed while making sure they had
taken their medicine for the night. Then, it was back to the soccer
practice to pick up her children.

When I started working with the senior care industry, I saw

many gals in the same boat as this mother. Some even called me in tears, begging for a solution.

The reason I share their stories is because this was the background that propelled me to get involved with social media marketing: on-line is where the gals of the aging parents were. As I mentioned in Chapter One, they are sitting in front of their computers at night in tears trying to find some way to ease their pain of being sandwiched with all their commitments.

I thought podcasting would add value to people's businesses and that they might even pay cold, hard cash for my services. I knew very little about social media: very little to say the least. Except for LinkedIn, which I had been using to market my podcasting and to find key people to interview as my guests on my shows.

I had two shows by January 2011: Eldercare 911 and Talent Management. Talent Management was a show to help retirement communities and others to find entertainment for seniors. I would interview performers, write a blog post and host them on my website.

I perform for seniors myself and knew that the senior living communities were always looking for entertainment. So, I thought this would be a nice side business. I am still performing for seniors today. I love them and they love me. We hand dance, sing, and shed a few tears together - happy tears! It does my heart good to sing with these wonderful people. They make me feel like I am singing to my own mother and father whom I miss very much.

Now, getting back to my show, with each guest I would add my introduction and conclusion (with music overlay) edit their interview, write a blog post about them and publish it on my pod blog site Eldercare 911. This site was set up so when a podcast was published, a message was sent out instantly to my Facebook, Twitter, LinkedIn, iTunes, and four different podcast sites.

As you can see, a large portion of my time is spent creating social media marketing for clients who pay for my efforts. I'm also attending networking meetings two to three times a week and conducting podcast interviews every Friday. These interviews take anywhere from two to eight hours to edit and publish. I listen to each interview again and again to edit out all the bloopers and some of the "umms" and "ahhs". Then, I add my professional intro and outro with music overlay and write a blog post about each person. Their headshot is attached to the blog along with the polished recording of their interview. I then send the published URL to each person for them to use on their website or to attach to their signature line of their email or however they choose to use it. Then, I post them through my social media (Sprout Social auto responder) so they appear on all my platforms once a month.

After Eldercare 911, the Marketing Mentress was born in January 2011. I started interviewing key business people and professionals and publishing those interviews on my two sites: www.practicalpodcasting.com and www.marketingmentress. podbean.com.

I discovered that I had to have a system for my interviews on my Marketing Mentress show. I had to offer massive value to people so they would appreciate the opportunity of being on my show and understand the true value for them and their businesses. .

There are the some points I created for my podcasting process.

Here they are:

I combined a list of questions (that I would be asking during the interview) to help prepare both of us for the interview. As their interviews were all about business, there were always marketing questions.

All of my interviews are done over Skype; I found that was the best for quality and investment. Free is always good.

Once the interview was completed, I did the editing.

The interview with the blog post and a headshot was published on my two sites.

I forwarded the published URL to my guest and they decided how they would like to use it.

The published podcast is then posted to all my social media once a week for the next four weeks, then once a month until the end of the year.

Finally, I write a recommendation for them on LinkedIn. From my experience, I noticed people in business are usually short on recommendations. Business coaches suggest that you ask those you have done business with to give you a recommendation. Well, I never could bring myself to ask. For me, asking people for a recommendation always makes me feel subservient. Plus, I receive requests from people regularly and I feel offended and sad for them at the same time. I can't write a professional recommendation because we haven't done business together.

So, I started being proactive. Now, after someone has been a guest on my show and if I feel comfortable, I'll write a recommendation. I started writing recommendations for everyone I have done business with on LinkedIn and do you know what? LinkedIn asks them to write one back, as soon as they have accepted it. Isn't that amazing? To this day, I have never asked for a recommendation and I have received many through LinkedIn.

The following are some of the tools I use to build my reputation on social media.

I send everyone a thank you card. It seems nobody sends "snail mail" any more and I wanted to stand out. I've been to business meetings where people have pulled out one of my thank you cards and showed it to everyone, exclaiming, "Look what the Marketing Mentress sent me!" I put their picture in the card, their company logo, and a special note of thanks. Sometimes I even send a gift. My cards have been written up in people's blogs and posted on Facebook, LinkedIn, and Twitter. My guests always send me a note via email or social media to thank me for their wonderful, personalized card: some even give me a phone call.

When was the last time someone sent you a thank you card in the mail?

From my shows I was meeting a lot of people and I truly believe that people show up in your life for a purpose. There's a reason why we meet the people we do. That has been my truth. I found myself hiding in my office just doing social media; therefore, it was purely by accident that I started going to networking meetings.

As I was meeting great people through LinkedIn, if they were local we would meet in person before I would arrange to do a podcast interview for having a chat over a coffee or tea helps to break the ice. One day I had a meeting with a gentleman at The Buzz Café in Vancouver, BC. Our meeting was set for eight o'clock in the morning. In order to get to my appointment, I needed to have use of our family car. I got up at four thirty in the morning to get ready and ride into Vancouver with my husband. Then I could use the car for the day.

Well, my husband has to be at work shortly after six-thirty in the morning, so that made me very early for my appointment, which wasn't until eight o'clock. We parked the car in my husband's free parking spot and then I walked six blocks to the Buzz Café. (After that first meeting, it became a routine, as that is where I would schedule all my meetings.) When I arrived at The Buzz Café, I could hear a hum from up above. Plus, there was a very long line up of people waiting to get their coffee before they went upstairs. I asked one of the women in the line-up what was going on? She said, "Oh! This is HOBN, High Output Business Network. Why don't you come up and join us?" Well, I had heard of HOBN a few years ago and had attended a few meetings. I had almost forgotten about the group. I decided to grab my breakfast and go upstairs to see what all the excitement was about. You know, curiosity gets the cat. Wow - was I impressed!

The room was filled with over forty people. They were all sitting around the room watching a presentation on the new

HOBN website that was being launched. As I sat and watched the presentation people greeted me and I felt welcomed and at home, but it was the website that caught my attention. The HOBN website was much like the LinkedIn platform I had become acquainted with over the past couple of years.

Then it was time for my eight o'clock appointment and I had to leave the meeting early. I was determined to make a point of attending their meeting again the following week. I went and once again I was so impressed and everyone was so friendly. You have no idea how much I needed to feel accepted and welcomed at this point in my life. It felt great and I knew I had come home. I was sold on the group and signed up that day. I haven't looked back since. I have grown to love all the members and guests that attend HOBN. I call the guys my "Teddy bear brothers" and the gals my "Barbie doll friends"! You can check them out at: www.hobnonline.com.

As you can see, because I arranged to meet a client at a coffee shop one day I went from working at home in my office to meeting an inspirational group of people.

Wow! And I have had the honour and privilege of having some of those dynamic people as guests on my show. As I mentioned earlier, each individual became my mentor in some way. A few of them asked me what they could do to return the favour. Isn't that amazing? I would say 20% of the people who were guests on my show offered to return the favour. It was with these kind people that I was able to work out some great trades.

As time went on I decided to trade my podcasting services for some great coaching. Even today, every time I interview someone on my show it's like I'm having a private coaching session. From these interviews I have gleaned life-changing advice from key business and life coaches who have helped me navigate through my journey of business and personal growth. Most of them don't even realize they have helped me in that way… oh, yes, they received their heart-felt thank you card!

These wonderful coaches helped me to find my voice, my confidence, and to realize that being pink-slipped wasn't just about me. They helped me to create a vision for myself; see what my true strengths are; and how to set and reach for my goals. In the following pages I'm going to share some insights from these wonderful coaches.

One of those coaches was Sheryl Stanton. Through Emotional Freedom Technique (EFT), Sheryl Stanton helped me to free myself of the past obstacles that were holding me back and causing me to be ill. She helped to relieve stress in my life (as a result of past programming) and recognize how it was affecting me today. I felt a lot of stress due to my present situation and it was going to make me very ill in the future if I didn't get it under control.

I never would have considered EFT before I met Sheryl Stanton. I thought it was a bunch of "Voo-Doo". I met Sheryl at a senior's fair that I had facilitated when I was working with the senior care agency. After we met, she started sending me her newsletters and invitations to her information sessions. As I read these emails, I became more and more curious about EFT. Soon I invited Sheryl to be my guest on my show.

Sheryl was most pleased to be invited and we scheduled her debut. In the interview Sheryl shared her incredible journey of her own serious illness: an illness she was told she would have to live the rest of her life with.

As Sheryl shared her life journey I also learned about her principles. Sheryl is a registered nurse with many years of experience, so for me that gave validation to the treatment. I became extremely curious and wanted to try it out for myself. You see, I have been extremely ill myself; I nearly died twice and both times I was blessed to have the same doctor who I will be forever grateful for saving my life. There was definitely a divine hand involved in this sequence of events.

From my life experience I believe stress can kill. We need to be aware of its influence and learn how to take care of ourselves. I am sharing these details because it may help you to understand why I was so curious about EFT and why I wanted to find out how I could stave off ever getting critically ill again. I knew I was under a tremendous amount of stress once again. I was a walking time bomb and I wanted to be proactive.

When the interview was over, Sheryl was pleased as punch with her finished product and posted it everywhere. Then, she sent me an email after our podcast inviting me to one of her "Stress Relief for Life" workshops that was being held in a local seniors community lecture hall.

Well, since it was being held in a senior's community hall I felt very comfortable attending. I was used to visiting these communities from my past job. The cost was about twenty dollars and I just couldn't pass it up.

About 30 people attended and Sheryl put us through some simple routines of EFT. I could feel that tapping on certain pressure points (the head, face, and hands) made total sense to me, as I was familiar with the pressure point technique from my massage therapist and chiropractor.

The next step was to attend a two-day workshop where I could learn how to do this for myself, but I couldn't afford to pay for it. After thanking Sheryl I went home thinking I wouldn't ever be able to have a chance to learn this technique. Well surprise, surprise. Who should phone me a few days later? Sheryl Stanton. She offered to trade her EFT healing sessions for my podcasting and LinkedIn training. Sheryl could see the stress I was under so she offered to help me.

We have been working together for the last year and she has done wonders to help relieve the stress in my life. I would have never believed it myself if I hadn't tried it, but here I am still going great guns with Sheryl helping me. We are trading; I coach her with her LinkedIn and social media marketing for her EFT sessions.

Thank you Sheryl, for loving me enough and sharing your gift of healing. I asked Sheryl to contribute to this book to help other people who are going through a similar situation and may be suffering from stress as a result.

Sheryl was happy to contribute.

You ARE Responsible but are You Response - Able?

This might sound a little harsh to say to someone who has lost their job and are facing financial security at an age when many people are thinking of retirement. I have been there myself. For 13 years I was the regional director for a Japanese student home-stay company in charge of all of Canada, plus Washington and Oregon. It was a very responsible, prestigious, well-paying job. I enjoyed it and was very good at it.

However, as the economy changed, the number of students slowly decreased each year. I should have seen the writing on the wall and prepared myself, but I didn't. At the age of 52 my position was phased out and my present financial situation was in absolute chaos, let alone my financial future.

I heard a motivational speaker say, "You are responsible for exactly the way your life is right now - good or bad." I remember being so angry. I said, "If I was a small child, how could I possibly be responsible for what happened to me then? Or what about a person who was a passenger in a car and is now paralyzed? Are they responsible?"

You might be thinking, "I haven't any control over the economy and I don't own the company. How am I responsible for the fact that I no longer have a job?"

In all of these examples, those things are just events. Sometimes we haven't any control over events that have happened in our lives - especially when we were children, but we need to realize it's not the event that causes our problems.

If it was, then everyone who experienced the same or a similar event would have the same problems: and we know that just isn't so. There are many people who have experienced horrible events in their past that have happy, healthy, productive lives today.

We may not be responsible for the event, but we are completely responsible for how we respond to that event. I have a personal story that demonstrates this.

My fourth son, David, was born with a rare form of Muscular Dystrophy that left him severely handicapped physically. This was probably the hardest thing I had to accept in my life. I'm a doer and a fixer and I'm also a nurse, but I couldn't do anything. I couldn't fix my son. For three years I fought the reality of David's situation constantly and asking why? "Why God? Why my son? Why me?"

It was driving me crazy: Until one day I realized there weren't any answers to my questions. As I see it, just asking them spirals you down into despair.

The reason "why" didn't matter. What mattered was what I was going to do about it. I was responsible for how I was going to handle this event in my life.

You have the same challenge now. It doesn't matter how or why you lost your job. It doesn't matter whose fault it is. The only thing that matters is what you are going to do about it. The first thing you have to do is to stop playing the "Blame Game".

This is probably the most common game played in the world and I was a past master at it. This is where you blame everyone and everything else for your problems. "It's not my fault that I'm out of work, sick, unhappy, broke, addicted... it's my parent's fault, my husband's fault, my boss's, the government's, God's, the devil made me do it..." We know them all and we use them.

The problem with this kind of thinking is that if it's someone else's fault, that makes you the victim; thus, powerless to do anything about it. As long as you blame someone else you will never be able to solve the problem.

The only way for your life to get better is to accept that you are responsible. Again, not necessarily for the event, but for how you respond to the event.

It's hard to do, but when you can accept that fact, it's the most powerful feeling in the world because if you're responsible for the problem - then you also have the ability to solve it.

There is a short story by Portia Nelson that demonstrates this.

"An Autobiography in 5 Short Chapters"

Chapter 1: I walk down the street. There is a deep hole in the sidewalk. I fall in. I am lost. I am helpless. It isn't my fault. It takes forever to find a way out.

Chapter 2: I walk down the street. There is a deep hole in the sidewalk. I pretend I don't see it. I fall in again. I can't believe I am in the same place, but it isn't my fault. It still takes a long time to get out.

Chapter 3: I walk down the street. There is a deep hole in the sidewalk. I see it there. I still fall in. It is a habit. My eyes are open. I know where I am. It is my fault. I get out immediately.

Chapter 4: I walk down the street. There is a deep hole in the sidewalk. I walk around it.

Chapter 5: I walk down a different street.

You see the person always had the ability to walk down a different street, but until she recognized that she was responsible for what happened to her, she did not have the power to do so.

Are You Response - Able?

Once you can accept the first part of your statement that you are responsible, you are then ready for the second part of the statement: but are you "Response - Able?"

"Response – Able" means: able to respond differently.

Most people are not "Response – Able" because they aren't even aware of why they are doing what they are doing. The truth is; most of us don't think very often.

Once we have learned to do a routine task, we don't think any longer of how to do it. This learning can be called programming or conditioning. We have established routines for how we do things. Just try to put your socks on a different foot and see how uncomfortable that feels.

We do most things automatically, without thinking. This is actually a good thing because if we had to consciously think about how to do everything every single minute we would go crazy - and nothing would get done.

Along with learning how to dress, walk, eat, and talk, we also learned ways of thinking and behaving that worked when we were helpless children.

As children we don't have many options and we have to accept what happens to us. We may have been conditioned emotionally to react in ways that aren't any longer in our best interest. They could actually be blocking our growth and be a bad thing.

How does this conditioning work?

First, you need to realize that we each have an invisible filter around us. It's used to filter every stimulus we are exposed to: every sight, sound, touch, taste, and feeling.

This perception filter will compare what we are looking at; for example, to see what it means in relation to what we already know to be true. Instantly, what we are looking at is compared to every other experience that we have ever had since our conception.

The purpose is to see if there is anything we have ever experienced that is remotely similar to what we are looking at. If there is, the same meaning will be assigned to what we are looking at now: good or bad, right or wrong, correct or incorrect.

Our perceptions are based on our values, our beliefs, and our early childhood conditioning, which, unfortunately, from what I've witnessed for most of us, was negative.

The actress and author, Shirley MacLaine said: "We see that world not as it is, but as we are."

Let's say a person was downsized, if their early childhood conditioning included a lot of criticism and rejection, they could have a perception filter that they're not good enough, smart enough or capable of succeeding. The event of losing their job would go through their perception filter and because of the negative programming, it could be translated as "I am a failure; I'm washed up; I'm not good enough".

Because of their conditioning, they could react in different ways. They might withdraw, either physically (reclusive) or emotionally (depressed). They might start comforting themselves with a variety of addictions: drugs, drinking, or overeating. They might get aggressive and either verbally or physically attack what they perceive as their enemy.

But the response to being downsized could be much different for someone who didn't have this same negative emotional conditioning. When it happened to me, I wondered what opportunity is coming? This is my chance to go back to school; do what I always wanted; there's a better job just waiting for me. I am really good at what I do; maybe it's time to start my own business and so on.

What is a negative emotional block or conditioning? Negative emotional conditioning is the conditioning that causes a person to negatively respond automatically to a certain emotional trigger. When the person perceives the trigger, (it can be any of the senses: sight, sound, touch, smell, taste) they are conditioned to respond the way they did when the negative emotional block was first created. They are not "Response – Able": not able to respond differently because of their negative conditioning.

An example could be someone who is a pleaser, who always does what others want and never stands up for themselves. They might have learned to respond as a pleaser because it was the only way they received love, approval or a degree of safety in an emotionally cold or abusive home. It was the right response at the time because they survived. But now, years later, if they are still responding as that frightened, insecure child - never speaking up, never expressing their needs, being a doormat, they are getting results they don't want.

Why can't people just go in and eliminate it? They can, once they know the negative emotional blocks are there. But, most of our conditioning was done before the age of understanding. We were too young to remember. We don't know why we do things we don't want to do or don't do things we do want to do, getting results we don't want to have.

That's why traditional "talk therapy" isn't all that effective. Talk therapy deals with the conscious mind and the conscious mind is like the tip of the iceberg. It really doesn't know very much. The subconscious mind knows it all, but it has buried all kinds of emotional stuff because it was too painful for us to handle.

How do you know if you have negative emotional blocks or conditioning in your life? Just look at your results. If you are not being, doing or having what you want in any areas in your life (your health, wealth, relationships, happiness, performance, etc.) there is a negative emotional block that is stopping you.

I tell people to check to see if they are experiencing any of the six 'U's -- Unhappy, Unhealthy, Unfulfilled, Unproductive, Unprofitable or Unfit to live with.

For many people, they have experienced the same problem over and over again. How many people have recycling financial crises? How many people have failed relationships again and again? How many people go from job to job to job? Until the underlying negative emotional block is eliminated, nothing is going to change in your life.

We spend all our time trying to change the externals of our lives; never realizing that the externals are just a reflection of the internal negative conditioning. When that is cleared away, the external results will fall into place and we will start to see the changes we've always wanted.

Where are these negative emotional blocks stored in the body? For over 5,000 years the Chinese have said that we had an energy system made up of microscopic energy vessels that they call Meridians. When the energy vessels are clear, our energy flows smoothly and easily. We are happy, healthy and energetic. Our life flows smoothly and productively; however, negative emotional conditioning can cause blocks that stop the energy from flowing freely. It might be helpful to picture these emotional blocks looking like blood clots in blood vessels.

The majority of people have negative emotional conditioning from their childhood that has interfered with the proper flowing of their body's energy for their entire life. If left unresolved, these emotional clots can contribute to health problems.

How do you get rid of negative emotional conditioning or blocks?

Of all of the energy therapies I studied in more than eight years of research, the most effective tool I found for breaking negative emotional blocks is Emotional Freedom Technique (also called EFT or Tapping).

EFT is like acupuncture, only you don't use needles. Instead you tap your fingertips on the ends of the body's main energy meridian points while focusing on whatever problem is bothering you. The tapping compresses the microscopic tubules between the bone of your fingers and the bone of the body part you are tapping on.

The tapping creates a vibration of the energy tubule, causing the emotional "clots" related to what you are tapping on to vibrate as well. This vibration actually breaks off and dissipates the emotional clots related to the problem you are focusing on.

It sounds completely weird and new agey, but it's based on science and it's incredibly effective. It gave me back my own health and happiness and in the seven years since I have been using it as a stress relief specialist: I have seen it create miracles in the lives of my clients.

What can you use EFT on? EFT can be used on anything you can think of. Any fear or phobia, anxiety and panic attacks, post traumatic stress disorder, depression, addictions, self-esteem or performance issues, relationship or money problems, any physical condition.

I encourage anyone who is facing a major change in his or her life to really look at what has happened and see if there is a pattern. If there is, it's very possible there is a negative emotional block, which is interfering with you being, doing or having what you want in life.

When you find yourself in the midst of a crisis, you are either on the edge of disaster or the verge of a miracle. You are responsible for what happens to your life. I hope that you will examine your life carefully to see if you are "Response-Able". If you are not, I encourage you to find someone that can help you remove the negative emotional blocks that are interfering with your quality of life. By learning to use a tool like EFT or having a skilled EFT Practitioner help you, you can be, do, and have what you want in life.

Sheryl Stanton is a registered nurse, Stress Relief

Specialist, EFT practitioner, author, speaker and trainer. In 2010, she received the "Woman of Worth" Health and Wellness Award. In 2011, she was chosen as the "Outstanding Professional of the Year in the Field of Stress Management Coaching" by Donald Trump Jr.'s Cambridge "Who's Who" Directory. For more information, go to www.SherylStanton.com

Another coach, Monika Becker, helped me to free myself from the grief and loss of losing my job. I found her on LinkedIn and was very interested in what she did when I read her profile. We also traded podcasting and LinkedIn coaching for her coaching sessions.

Through her coaching I was able to realize that I was a good person and that the most important people loved me in my life; namely my Heavenly Father, my husband and my family. I have even learned to love myself.

It's amazing how situations from my childhood cropped up in our coaching sessions. I had forgotten all about being called "the witch" in school and not having friends. Monika helped to bring it up, to talk about it, and I learned to deal with those feelings in a simple, holistic way. I learnt many things; for example, I learnt not to hold grudges against others or feel hurt by them any longer; past loves, money patterns, and how I think about money. In regards to money, I discovered I didn't feel I deserved to be wealthy because of all these things from my childhood. We continue to work on these challenges to this very day.

What a treat it is working with Monika. She has been one of the many people who has helped me to find my voice. Concurrently, she has given me tools to strengthen my mind and spirit: she helped me build my self-esteem and she helped me to feel good about myself. Also, through working with Monika, I gained the confidence and inspiration to start writing my book.

Thank you, Monika, for your gift of believing and hope. You

can connect with Monika through her website:
www.cleardirections.ca

Carolyn Cooper-McOuatt inspired me to rise up to my true
potential and have the courage to ask for business. I met Carolyn
on LinkedIn as well. I was attending all these networking meetings
and every time I would give my elevator speech I would sit down
without asking for anything. Carolyn was attending some of
these meetings with me and she listened to me doing this time
and again.

We created a different kind of pilot project together. We did a
series of podcasts where she spoke about the different modules
in her Inspired Living Business Plan. Carolyn radiates true caring
and love for each of her clients. One day she invited me over to
her home for a visit. It was during this visit that she shared with
me how I could ask by inviting people. I thought to myself, I can
do that. Carolyn does not know this, but I cried tears of joy as
I was driving back to my home that day. To think that someone
really cared enough to sit and tell me what a wonderful, special
person I was and what I had to offer is so unique. She confirmed
her belief by stating that people really needed to be able to learn
how to use LinkedIn the way I use LinkedIn. She inspires me to
laugh and be the sanguine I am: and be proud of it.

What a great time we have had together. The first time I sang a
jingle at one of our HOBN meetings Carolyn yelled and cheered
for me. I could hear her voice above all the others who were also
clapping and cheering. Carolyn helped me to open my mouth
and ask for what I want. Thank you, Carolyn, for your gift of
love and friendship.

I asked Carolyn to contribute to my book so my readers could
benefit from her wisdom; here is how Carolyn Cooper McOuatt
helped me. Thank you, Carolyn!

Leading for Legacy
"Live Above the Line" - *from mediocrity to greatness*
Everyone Has a Story!

I have lived a life of yearning for the keys to happiness, looking up at every star wishing that I could find the answers. My entire life has been an expedition of discovery, surrender, courage, humbleness, love, and faith. Each hurdle, wall, obstacle, and challenge has been a learning experience of truth and realization. As I look back at my 54 years I appreciate each encounter of certainty and will continue my exploration with an open mind and heart. Each day I discover characteristics about myself from my family, friends and clients that teach me to be real, genuine and authentic. I know that this time around is about consistently being curious with a vast sense of wonder as to what is, what can be and feeling the energy of enthusiasm as we bring our dreams into reality.

My childhood was one of searching for joy in life because I saw the pain that my mother lived in and the lack of support she created around herself. She was diagnosed when I was a teenager with schizophrenia and then I knew I held the responsibility of my family. I became an over achiever. As I moved into my 20's I realized my ticket to freedom was understanding people and what motivated them to make decisions and take action. I was successful at sales and created financial abundance. I became bored and had a hunger in my soul to find out what else there was in life and business to adventure into. At 30 I decided to take a giant leap and go to Europe (which I had always dreamed of experiencing). I let go of everything I had known with all the comforts of my home, money and family and I quit my job and left. I traveled extensively on my own to many countries and met great people. When I came back, I moved to Vancouver to learn what I did not know about business and life.

What I have learned is what is really important in life and in my business is that love is the most powerful healing force of all. I have realized that everyone has a story that they tell themselves that keep them from achieving their dreams and they play small because of it. We all hold on to this story to keep safe, not go for what we want and hide. It limits so many of us from stepping into our greatness.

What life has taught me is that we all have excruciating stories in our lives that we can articulate with crystal clear authority and description. Our stories play over and over in our minds and over time it becomes who we are rather than something that has happened, an event. What I know is that my story of my witnessing the pain that my mother went through with her mental illness became my search for answers to help her. It became my search for meaning and purpose. I needed to let go of the anger, blame and resentment first with forgiveness for her and myself. Then it became my purpose and passion to live by and lead by what I had learned from my mentors, wise women. I decided to change my story in my mind with the learning and research I had discovered. What I realized is that the character in each of us is influenced by the pain we have experienced and we have an opportunity to find a purpose to lead by and it becomes our passion fuel. For me this concept became a source for authority, a source of inspiration and dedication of discipline which has allowed me to see the joy, experience gracious gratitude and resource the love deep inside of me to share that with my beloved family, friends and communities that I serve. It has been an expedition of courage, one of strong faith and conviction to find the solutions in each moment regardless of the severity of the obstacle in front of me. I am no longer a victim to anything, any person or situation. I have defined this blueprint as "Live Above the Line"; leading a life from mediocrity to greatness. This wisdom is the foundation of all that I stand for and lead by as I inspire business leaders to step up to the same position as they become strong leaders in their industry. They contribute with more clarity, conviction and focus. We collaborate together to design a new vision, direction and strategy for growth and profits; change their story to build for a new future to lead their legacy with a foundation of making a remarkable difference.

I know that we are all the same in this regard and that those old stories that we play over and over and over again are not who we are. The truth is we are all destined for greatness if we are willing to see the wisdom in the story and be humbled enough to discover the knowledge we can resource to be the leader we came here to be; to be Leading for Legacy.

There have been mentors that have made a deep impact on my life. They have supported, guided and lead me to be clear on what is most important, to be bold, have great courage, to hold onto faith even when there is no evidence at hand, to take action anyway and love with all my heart.

One of my mentors was Emma Smiley. She was a woman who saw in me so much and what I did not. She was in her 80's when I was in my 20's. She gave me a golden key that has meant so much to me over the years. It is the symbol of my business – the key to your business dreams, potential and profits. The key has provided strength, meaning, clarity and grounded energy for me when I have taken big risks in my life and business.

Emma and I would go for lunch and I would listen to her stories and know that my life was somehow being transformed. Her message was one of truth, kindness, love and gracious gratitude. She celebrated with me every win I had and taught me that we needed to realize that our accomplishments truly made such a big difference in the world not only for us but also for others. I remember being shocked the way she looked at me as I told her about how much I had sold in beauty supply products. She would say, "Think of all those people feeling so beautiful". I thought - Wow I guess that is true, I better sell some more and help more people feel that way. So I did, again and again and again. She helped me to realize it was not the product that was important; it was about how people felt as they experienced it. She bought face cream from me and asked me how much younger she looked using it. I can tell you honestly there was not much difference as far as I could see. She was 83 and she glowed which is all that matters.

Each time we met I would learn about the principles of - Thinking above the line (her short book). I felt like a blossoming flower and butterfly each time I left thinking about what could be possible for me in my life's adventure. She would talk only about the good and bring every conversation to focus on solution and the contribution to situations. I knew I was blessed to have such positive seeds planted in my soul for me to water for my future growth. I loved being in her presence with her gracious, positive, gentle, kind energy and glowing spirit. I looked at her as my adopted mother as my mother suffered with her mental illness challenges. Emma was like a ray of sunshine and provided to me an example of what I dreamed of being one day. She died when I was 26 and that day I knew that it was my job to lead her legacy.

I have taken her principles to heart and continued to be open to learn the depth of those truths. I have taught what she shared with me to thousands of eager entrepreneurs who wanted direction, support and guidance. I created a chart to share the principles and to guide me to make choices each day to "Live above the line" and let go of the thoughts of living below the line.

The three keys to Live above the line are: Wonder, Curiosity and Enthusiasm

The three elements of Living below the line are: Skeptical, Critical and Stuck

Each day I think of, speak about and share the value of Living Above the Line and it reminds me of the power of an open mind, an open heart, to come from a place of contribution, to take risks and step up with courage and faith, to dream big and be clear on what I desire, to know that we are all here to move forward and make a meaningful difference to create loving relationships.

My client's business development inspires and teaches me. I have had the honor to guide and lead them to grow their businesses to the next level of contribution, next level of profits and to higher levels of fulfillment.

Suzanne Kanina's story is one of amazing courage, internal strength, faith and vision. She has inspired me over the years and I know she will inspire you as you hear her story. I met her in 2002 after her partner came to present to my husband and I and we made the choice to move our financial management over to their company. She came from being on welfare with two children as a single mother, to working in the office with administrative functions. I started coaching her to keep expanding her role in the company. I witnessed her stepping up with courage and conviction time and time and time again. She has consistently chosen to Live Above the Line and takes bold risks with faith. Her ability and strength to hold her vision for what she wanted and to manifest it in a short time was amazing to witness. There were aspects of her dreams that she thought were impossible and with Living Above the Line focused energy she made them a reality. At one time it was an impossibility that she would live with her partner let alone live in her dream home. She created a contrast (details of what she did not want in a home), clarity list (details of exactly what she wanted in the home). Within a short time she walked into her dream home and called me to come and see it. I was shocked when I saw that this home was exactly to the letter what she had listed on her clarity list and she moved in with her partner and her two children. With each new challenge she continued to learn, step up, show up and speak up with a voice of confidence. She gradually moved into a sales Live Above the Line position and began to shine providing memorable customer service that her clients raved about. One day she woke up on a Monday morning and found her partner had passed. Her life had changed in an instant. She realized that she needed to grieve and redefine her life and her new dreams. She decided to create her vision for the business with a strong purpose and passion to serve her clients that she did with honour for her partner. She became strong in the ability to let go to lead and to Live Above the Line. She has become a bold woman in business and a leader and pioneer in the financial industry, running a successful team of professionals and a profitable business.

Another client that has taken the philosophy to heart and made great strides in her business development is a Spa owner. (Spa Divine, Shannon Morse - Port Moody, BC) She opened her business ten years ago with a big vision to support women to take time to nourish their mind, body and spirit. She is an advocate for women to love themselves so in turn that love can be shared with their families, friendships and communities they serve. She is an elegant example of what it is to be a woman of conviction, courage and grace. I have been a witness to her clarity development as a leader with her staff and clients. Each obstacle she has faced she has taken the time to consider the option of Live Above the Line and focus on a solution and take action. Her ability to surrender to the truth is inspiring and her strength to keep moving forward with dignity and grace fills my heart.

We women need to be vulnerable to lead. We need to be willing to look at the truth head on, deep in the center and let go. We have been given the gift of knowing what love is as we lead our legacy. Our legacy is the trail of love that we contribute to our families; each person we connect with and the seeds that we can impart that will make a difference in their lives. I believe our job is to live as a woman of wonder, staying open to what life has to teach us. Also, we need to come together to support each other to be bold, to step up, show up and speak up with a voice of clarity and conviction and strength.

Emma taught me so much at such a young age and she is still teaching me through the aspects of Live Above the Line. I know that this is the legacy that I want to leave my children and people I have touched. My legacy is to believe in possibilities, to hold a vision, live in the moment with love in your heart, keep taking risks and stepping out of your comfort zone and celebrate with gratitude for what you have.

Thank you to Emma for taking the time to connect and contribute to me and thank you to my mother for her courage to step up and lead from a place of love.

Carolyn Cooper-McOuatt
www.inspiredbusiness.ca
Carolyn@inspiredbusiness.ca

Next, entered… Julie Salisbury.
My publisher, Julie Salisbury, is a saint. She helped me to publish this book. Julie and I met at a women's club meeting called, "Dollar Makers". I was so impressed with her and her authors (who also attended) that I invited all of them to be my guests on my show. Little did I know that we would be working together on my own book.

One of the tools I have in my toolbox is lead generation, which I do through LinkedIn. Julie and I have been trading services. I help her with social media and lead generation to invite people to attend her live webinars. I wouldn't have been able to publish my book without her help.

One day, after Julie had been a guest on my show, she called me out of the blue to invite me to attend one of her Authors Circle Workshops. It was two days of intensive work shaping my book into what it would look and feel like. Let me tell you, when I came out of that workshop I had completely done a three-sixty. Before I met Julie, I had started writing my book and had been typing and typing. I was just rambling without much sense of order (I did have the sense to put together an outline) and get this; the title of my book was "Enhancing Your personal Marketability". Now, who in their right mind would buy that book?

Well, by the end of the first day I had thrown out my little outline and my title had changed to "Pink-slipped at 55". By the end of the second day, the title had changed to "Fired at Fifty". I left that workshop with my entire book laid out. Now all I had to do was sit down and write. I knew I would be able to compose a powerful book that would speak to my target audience (to help others who found themselves in the same position as me) and deliver my message with power and confidence.

Julie and all these wonderful coaches helped me to find my voice and the confidence to realize that being pink-slipped wasn't all about me. It helped me to create a vision for myself; to see what my true strengths were and how to set and reach for goals in my life.

Chapter Three

Break Through — Apply Your Skills

I had some experience as a business consultant and I knew a few things I needed to have in place for my business. A website was one, (with the use of a Wordpress platform) and with the help of Dick Low, a very good, inexpensive website pro, I was able to get my website up and running. I knew my website needed to be attractive and serviceable. It had to be able to convert (a website where people can go and pay for your products and services) to make money. I had to have a way for people to go into my website, book appointments, and pay through PayPal. Do you have a PayPal account set up yet? Simply go to www.paypal.com and set up your free business account today. It's simple, just follow the instructions on their website.

I attend many networking meetings and I still meet people who don't have a website. In today's world a website validates your business and you. It's a place for people to find out more about you and what you do. It's a place to offer products and services that people can order and pay for right on the spot. Your website can do all the heavy lifting to help you close sales.

Right off the bat I had Jonathan Christian, social media guru, as a guest on my show. His branding is: "We Make Stuff Happen". Do you know what? I found him through LinkedIn as well. It was an honour to take my first full day course in social media with Jonathan. The course was called Social Media 101. He helped me get my @mktgmentress Twitter account and my Google profile set up. He also taught me about the use of hash tags.

On Twitter, you can create a statement unique to yourself,

and add "#YourName" and you become someone who can be quoted for making that statement. Isn't that great? It's like publishing yourself a little at a time. Here is my favourite original statement: "My name is Christine Till, as in Till we meet again. Where there's a Till, there's a will, and where there's a will, there's a way!" #ChristineTill."

Jonathan Christian taught me this trick! Thank you, Jonathan. Periodically, Jonathan invites me to be a guest speaker during his workshops. His specialties are: Facebook, blogging, and setting up your social media program. LinkedIn isn't his specialty and that's why he invites me to share a few tips about LinkedIn at some of his workshops.

Neil Godin helped me realize the importance of having a website that could convert. I thought all I needed was to have a simple website and all the people who visited would just connect and order - I soon learned differently.

I have known Neil Godin for many years. We met through the Business Owner Development Program, a government funded small business training program that was funded federally. Neil and a team of trained speakers and experts travelled across Canada training small business owners. Neil was one of the professional speakers they brought in to speak about "Marketing Dangerously". I have learned a lot from Neil over the years and continue to learn today as we work together marketing his webinars and on-line training programs from time to time.

Neil teaches all of what we do on-line needs to be well thought out. What we do with our social media is directed to a landing page on our website, which then invites people to buy our special offer or register with a tuition for a seminar, webinar, and other products. Check out Neil's latest book "Selling in the (Comfort) Zone".

It has been an honour to have several social media gurus as guests on my show and they have taught me a wealth of knowledge about how to use social media. I have discovered this is an ongoing education. Social media is constantly changing; however, I had to keep it simple because I didn't have the time or the money to spend hours a day on my computer or to hire someone at seven hundred dollars a month to do it for me. What most of the social media mavens (a maven is an expert in some area, like with social media) will tell you that you need to have a presence on Twitter, Facebook, LinkedIn, YouTube, and Google+. Then you need to have a blog, which is the centre of your social media program. That's the bare bones to start off with. Today I have accounts on all five platforms. Where are you with your social media? What platforms are you using at present?

I then met the social media maven Bonnie Sainsbury. She stressed the importance of having a social media auto responder with great analytics. So acting on her advice, I started using Sprout Social (www.sproutsocial.com).

Now, with Sprout Social I know who is following me and where they come from on all my social media platforms. To this day, I use both Sprout Social and HootSuite platforms for my social media auto-responding. They each have their pros and cons.

HootSuite shows you all your social media streams on one platform. The second your message is posted, you can see exactly what is being posted to your Twitter, Facebook, and LinkedIn accounts. You can also respond to each of these platforms through your accounts on HootSuite which also has a great news feed. In my humble opinion, there are two things missing from HootSuite. The first is the fact that you can only post to schedule on one date at a time. Therefore, every time you want to repost something; for example, a workshop, you have to copy and paste it for every date you want to send it out. The second is the analytics: you can't see who your target market is.

I prefer to use Sprout Social because of the analytics and the ability to post to all my social media platforms (for multiple dates) at one click. It's also user-friendly as far as responding to direct posts (within the platform) that come to each of your social media accounts.

Another point that many social media mavens will teach is that you need to style your postings to each individual platform. Well, who has time for that?

I set up all my postings on my social media to fit Twitter (140 characters or less) and then it fits all my platforms. You see, when you use Sprout Social, the search engines read the URL that you attach to the post and the post automatically expands to fit Facebook and LinkedIn the instant it is posted. Modern technology is amazing, isn't it?

I needed to have a profile on Twitter, Facebook, LinkedIn, Google+ and YouTube, and have a blog. (My blog is my posts for my podcasts on my website, PracticalPodcasting.com) Now, what do I post on them? In all the social media articles I have read, the one thing they all have in common is that we need to have a plan. However, from what I've discovered, they never tell you how to put the plan together in a step-by-step process. I don't know about you, but I need to have steps; for example, Step One, you do this … Step Two, you do this … etc. They also don't advise you what to post. All they usually suggest is that it needs to be relevant to your business; what you do; and that your posts need to have massive value.

Another learning curve I had was recognizing the time I could save by using social media auto-responders. I was spending inordinate amounts of time sitting in my office composing and posting relevant articles as to what I do as The Marketing Mentress. After I completed a podcast interview, I would have to go to each of my individual social media platforms and post that pod-blog.

Now, lucky for me, there is a lot of information available that I can pull from the internet; however, unlucky for me, it kept me reading and researching constantly for 12 to16 hours a day. Do you have 12 to 16 hours a day to spend researching and learning what to do with your social media platforms and then how to implement it?

My poor family, especially my husband has paid the price with me spending excessive amounts of time in my office working on my social media. But, do you know what? I have been extremely blessed through all this time because my husband saw what I went through while I was working for Mr. No. I was almost burning myself out working full time during the day, while in the evenings I was working on podcasting. My husband witnessed how I was trying to prove the importance of being on-line when the children of seniors where searching for ways to ease their pain. My husband was happy as he wanted me to be working at home. He believed in me. He could see that I was onto something big and he just kept encouraging me to keep going and make my dreams come true.

What would be your biggest dream?

Let's go back to when I was still working for Mr. No for that is how I was able to identify one of my biggest dreams. The first year I was with the senior care company Mr. No took me to an annual event sponsored by their head office in the United States. He took me along to give me a better understanding of how the company worked and operated. Concurrently, he wanted me to learn and gather new information to assist me with my marketing efforts for his franchise. I was excited to be there because I also wanted to be able to do the best marketing job I could for this company. I desperately wanted to be a great asset to my boss.

It was an intense week of networking and training in all the areas of operating a franchise. There were several sessions for those involved with marketing (from the different franchises) and I thoroughly enjoyed these. On the last day everyone was invited to a presentation to be given by Mary Kaye (not the make-up entrepreneur) and there were approximately 500 people in the room.

The franchise owners were invited to attend another meeting;

therefore, Mr. No didn't see what happened. Mary Kaye spoke about keeping a positive mental attitude and how to build our own personal self-esteem. She also shared her personal story of how she rose from poverty to where she is now. Mary came to a point in her presentation where she invited us to turn to the person sitting beside us and share what our big dream was and how it would feel once we accomplished it.

I was sitting in an aisle seat, so I turned to my left, but the gal on my left was already speaking with the person beside her. I looked right, across the aisle, thinking I would just walk over there to the person on the end. Well, she was also engaged in conversation with the person next to her. I looked around to see if there was anyone else, but everyone was chatting. I sat there and started saying to myself, "My dream is to…" when I was interrupted by Mary Kaye herself. She kneeled beside my desk and asked me what my dream was. I was tickled pink and immensely nervous all at the same time! Imagine that? Mary Kaye came to speak to me! I said my dream was to sing for seniors. She asked me if I had any voice training and I told her that I had been singing and performing since I was three years old and was classically trained. Then, later on as an adult I had directed music at church. Then she asked me how it would feel when I accomplished my dream? Before I could answer, she realized the time was up and had to run back up to the stage. What a rush! I was so tickled that Mary Kaye had noticed me.

Mary Kaye then did something I would never have dreamt of in a million years. First she elicited from everyone if they had shared their dream and how it would feel when they accomplished it. What happened next had me almost fall out of my chair. Mary Kaye asked me (yes me) to come up to the stage and share my dream with the entire audience. I got up there and she handed me the microphone. Well, my palms were suddenly sweaty and the microphone stuck to my fingers, my mind went into a blur, but I composed myself and proudly announced, "My dream is to sing with seniors." Then, Mary Kaye asked me how it would feel when I had accomplished my dream? I almost lost it right there in front of 500 people, but managed to retain my composure.

I responded with, "I would be in a room full of seniors clapping and cheering. Those in electrical wheelchairs, who could not clap or speak, would be moving their steering sticks back and forth making their chairs go ee-oo-ee-oo, and I would be standing in front grinning from ear to ear with tears streaming down my cheeks."

You'll never guess what Mary did next. She asked me to sing a song for them, right there on the spot! I tried to mumble that I didn't have any music with an accompanist, or me but she said, "Just sing whatever pops into your head."

Well, I remembered "You Are My Sunshine". Gosh, I hadn't sung that song since I was a little girl with my mom and two sisters. Together we had sung it at family reunions, church parties, and community gatherings. I started singing soprano and as I was singing, suddenly people in the audience were harmonizing with me. Talk about a memorable experience: This one took the cake. It was all I could do to keep myself from dissolving into tears on the spot. I sang one verse and stopped. Mary thanked me and I handed her my slippery, sticky microphone and sat back down. After the presentation, many people came up and complimented me on my singing.

Now, that same day before the evening banquet, there was a final seminar. We were all brought together (individual franchises) to set up our marketing plans for the following year. We took the week's training and sat around individual tables in a big room. Mr. No and I had just started writing down some of our ideas when the owner of the entire company approached us and told him about the wonderful experience he had listening to me sing. Mr. No didn't have any idea of what had transpired: He didn't know I could sing.

Later on during the big banquet, between the dinner and

the awards ceremony, I excused myself to duck into the ladies room and as I was standing in the proverbial line-up, women complimented me about my singing. Then one woman who approached me suggested, "That was totally planned, wasn't it?" There were several other women who nodded and echoed, "Yeah, we know, it was planned!" I quickly explained that I was from Canada and before the conference I didn't know Mary Kaye or the owners of the company - all the women in the entire line up sighed in surprise. You had to be there to understand the feeling I had as everyone felt the penny drop. Then, as I returned to my table from the ladies room where Mr. No and several other people were seated, some people came up to me (in front of Mr. No) and complimented me.

Where do you think my mind was by this time? You guessed it. I was on cloud nine. The following morning, as we were waiting in the airport to board the aircraft, I had more people approach me to compliment me about my singing. Now, there were people around us who hadn't heard me sing so they were wondering what had happened - and so was Mr. No by this time. I then related the story, just as I have shared with you. I wish I could have had a camera. You should have seen Mr. No's face. Well, nothing more was said at that time and we caught our flight home.

I could hardly wait to tell my husband. He hugged me and was so pleased for me. Little did he know what was coming next: I announced I was going to find a way to achieve my dream. I asked my husband if we could look for some kind of an amplifier and iPod that I could download music and plug into the amplifier to accompany me while I went around to all the different retirement villages and sang. He said that he would get that organized for me. That made my whole week! Woo-hoo! I was going to find a way to accomplish my dream!

The next morning I walked into the office early to speak with Mr. No. I wanted to tell him about my big idea. I believed I could do this for free to help market his franchise. Well, Mr. No surprised me. He said he would pay for whatever I needed and I could perform for seniors on the franchise's behalf: as community service. My big dream was coming true. Can you believe it? I had to run down the hallway because the tears of joy were welling up, and I didn't want to embarrass myself in front of Mr. No.

The very next day Mr. No had a big box to show me. He had found a portable amplifier and had purchased an iPod for me. I could have started singing on the spot. Together we read through all the instructions and figured out how everything worked and all I had left to do was download music from the Internet. I already knew a lot of the old songs that senior's love, so I just had to find the karaoke accompaniment on-line. That was the hard part. To this day, for some of the older songs, there just isn't any Karaoke music; however, thus began my singing career with seniors.

I believe there is always a reason we meet certain people in our lives: in certain places at certain times. If I hadn't been working for Mr. No and hadn't attended that seminar, perhaps I never would have been inspired to accomplish my dream of singing and getting fired led me to a different way of podcasting. See how life works? Beautiful, isn't it?

One day when I was in New Westminster for some appointments on behalf of Mr. No's company, I was walking down the street to where my car was parked and I met a man singing on a street corner. He was good! I stopped to ask him why he was singing on a street corner because he was really good. During our ensuing conversation he discovered that I was singing at retirement communities for seniors and asked if he could come and listen. He also asked if he could bring his partner along and that is how I met Nick Parsons. My husband and I went over to Nick's home to audition him for his piano prowess. I was impressed, so I invited Nick to be my guest on my Talent Management podcast show. That interview is on my Memro Talent website.

Today Nick and I entertain all over the Vancouver Lower

Mainland. I asked him to share some of his story. Nick has Aspergers. He is also referred to as a "music savant". He is a wonderful pianist.

Thank you, Nick for sharing your journey.

MY DREAM
My dream is that one day people will treat each other as equals. I hope one day when we accept others differences we will embrace and learn from others lives and experiences. I believe that by living life in another's shoes we will begin to see the diversity of experiences we can learn from others and appreciate their differences. We must teach ourselves to do this: no one can do it for us. It's only by our acceptance of differences that we will create a peaceful, more loving world. I have hope and faith that this dream will one day exist: this is my dream.

For the purpose of this article I will use people's initials in order to keep them anonymous.

MY FIRST YEARS
My challenges in life started when I was young. I was diagnosed with autism and Aspergers Syndrome (disorder). Autism is a disorder of neural development characterized by impaired social interaction and communication, and by restricted and repetitive behaviour. Asperger's disorder is an autism-spectrum disorder that is characterized by significant difficulties in social interaction, alongside restricted and repetitive patterns of behaviour and interests. It differs from other autism-spectrum disorders by its relative preservation of linguistic (language) and cognitive (brain) development.

As mentioned, autism (Aspergers) isn't just restricted to social factors, but also educational. Throughout my life, I have had a lot of learning and social challenges and barriers to cross and overcome. Along with my educational accommodations, I have always preferred to work independently and have had difficulty in getting involved in activities.

STARTING SCHOOL AND MUSIC

My main elementary school was T.E. Scott in Surrey, British Columbia. I spent six years there. When I first started school I was diagnosed with having difficulty in two principal areas, which affected my learning: reading comprehension and higher level thinking. Reading comprehension is the ability to understand or comprehend what one reads. Higher level thinking involves three parts: summarizing, to make a summary or express in concise form; synthesizing, to form by combining parts or elements; analyzing, to separate into component parts or elements.

Because of my learning impairments, I was put into the Learning Assistance Program, where I worked with A.M. and D.G. I was given help and accommodations for exams (including exam taking skills) and coursework. They also provided me with assistance in regard to planning and time management, and worked with me both inside and outside of the classroom (I was given help and assistance in another special room for students who were mentally and physically challenged).

I received many awards in elementary school, including music, math, and spelling. My favourite teacher there was M.B. whom I had for grade four. In grade seven (L.W. was my teacher) our class took a trip to Victoria. This trip led to new experiences for me, including the first time I had ever taken a ferry. We visited many locations, including many museums and art buildings and had lunch at Beacon Hill Park. For me, it was interesting to hear a bagpiper at one of the parks in Victoria as it reminded me of my own heritage. That trip had a big impact on me. Later on in grade seven a formal event was held for our class to celebrate our completion of grade (elementary) school and our transition to high school.

My music education started when I was four years old and since then I have studied with the Royal Conservatory of Music (RCM) for 26 years. I started out with group lessons at a music academy for the first few years before switching to private lessons. I have had a number of private music teachers, including C.L., N.G. and S.A. It was discovered shortly after I started music that I have absolute pitch. Absolute pitch (commonly called perfect pitch) is the ability of a person to identify or re-create a given musical note without the benefit of an external reference. Eight years later I started teaching music when I was 12 years old and since that time I have had a variety of students over the years, from children to seniors.

ADOLESCENCE/TEEN YEARS

I went to Tamanawis Secondary School, Surrey, B.C., and was a graduate of the class of 2000. Apart from the core subjects, I majored in business and took many accounting and computer courses. One of my favourite classes in high school was accounting in grade 11. Our teacher J.H., always made us laugh.

Much like elementary school, in high school I was in the learning assistance program (at the time called CELD). I worked with several special needs teachers in and outside of the classroom. My assistance included planning and time management, exam skills and accommodations, and assignment and coursework completion.

Not only was I a special needs student; I also worked with special needs students. Seeing things on both sides of the fence taught me many skills, such as the ability to see things from a different perspective and compassion for others. Working with those who are less fortunate is, in itself, very rewarding. I also developed respect and trust from other students and teachers.

INTO ADULTHOOD

After I graduated from high school I went to Kwantlen

University College. For my first year I was a music major in piano. Here I met J.F. a flute player who was studying at an advanced level. I was required at the end of the year to accompany an instrumentalist on a final song; thus I accompanied J.F. I have since kept in touch with J.F. and practice with him as often as I can.

After finishing a year of music, I switched majors and studied business and accounting. In 2002, I graduated with an accounting certificate in Applied Business Technology and Integrated Bookkeeping. In 2005 I graduated with an Accounting Diploma with an interest in computers. I took an advanced computers course and scored top marks.

My disability accommodations extended in Kwantlen and were similar to those in elementary and high school. I was given the use of a computer and extra time for exams, a note taker in class, and classroom accommodations.

I attempted the grade ten piano exam (for the third time) and achieved it with an honours standing, allowing me to work on material at the grade 11 (ARCT) level. Once I had achieved this level, it allowed me to focus on the emotional aspect of music and further connection and communication.

WAL-MART

After obtaining my Accounting Diploma I had difficulty in finding employment. Through a lead from one of my uncles, I was able to secure a job at Wal-Mart. I worked at Wal-Mart for almost five years (2006 - 2011). My main responsibility was working the front end, which required me to bring in buggies and do carry-outs, and, when needed, recovery (I wasn't trained on cash). I also assisted in the food and dairy departments and in receiving, where I unloaded inventory from the delivery trucks and brought the skids to the sales floor.

As a result of my physical duties, I injured my left leg by pulling my hamstring. I needed physiotherapy for many weeks and had to take time off due to the pain and soreness in my leg. I went back part time for six weeks on light duty. I only worked a few months when I resumed my regular duties at the front end before deciding to hand in my notice and leave. My choice to leave Wal-Mart was based on a number of factors; however, the fact was I wanted to go back to school and pursue my music full time. Also with the injury, I found it difficult to put stress on my left leg for a long period of time.

MY WEBSITE

Shortly after that I met a man, M.G., when he was playing music outside a local retail store. I told him about my music knowledge and training. We became friends and he worked with me to create a website to show my music skills in 2009. I use this site to show my musical knowledge, to market my skills and to network with other business professionals and musicians. I have also made business cards with the help of my mother. My website has always been a work in progress and will continue to be.

My website is:
www.musiceducationandcompositions.com.

MEETING CHRISTINE

Through a friend, my story of meeting Christine begins. My friend had met Christine and invited me to attend one of her performances. Soon after hearing her perform, I told her about my musical background. I then met her husband .

After meeting her husband, Christine interviewed me (www.jvexpert.podbean.com/2011/04/04/nick-parsons-on-piano/). We became friends and now Christine and I do part-time performances at local seniors centres and retirement homes. We both love it. We have been performing together since 2011 and our stage name is, "Till We Meet Again."

MUSIC

My music can be divided into several distinct areas: composing, performing, singing, piano playing (both classical and non-classical) and teaching. In regards to performing, I work with different vocalists at different senior's centres and retirement homes. I enjoy performing, as do the singers I work with and the residents who come to listen. They appreciate the music. I also perform for family and friends at gatherings and smaller functions.

My knowledge of classical training has allowed me to work at the grade 11 (ARCT) level with S.A. and continue to work fulfilling my advanced theory requirements. Also, S.A. and I are working on pieces for two pianos: four hands. This knowledge has also allowed me to compose my own musical works, both classical and non-classical.

My musical compositions include a wide variety of styles: military, pop/soft rock, hard rock, country rock, ballads, choral hymns, and orchestral. My ballads are generally love song duets (female and male voices), and use drums and light accompaniment (harp, piano, flute, etc.). I am also writing classical compositions from various eras, including Baroque, Classical, Romantic, and Impressionistic.

SCHOOLING

I plan to go back to school and obtain my music degree in vocal performance (also focusing on composition), and my Masters in Music Therapy. To obtain this degree in vocal performance, I will take instruction at a post-secondary level and/or outside lessons to help with various aspects of singing. I will likely take language courses as well. I would also love to obtain my PhD in neuroscience (possibly neurobiology). After graduating, I plan to work as a musical therapist, as well as open doors for other researchers in the field in regards to music therapy.

IN CLOSING…

"Life is like a box of chocolates,
you never know what your going to get"
Forest Gump

Nicholas Parsons
www.worldmusiceducationandcompositions.com

Now, from my life experience I would like to share some "Dos and Don'ts" with you. Have you ever made a total idiot of yourself in front of a bunch of people? When it came to building my business, I'm afraid I made plenty of mistakes. Being the fun-loving person that I am, I have made many "faux-pas" as I attended networking meetings and in reaching out to people through the many online systems. I have had to learn to keep my mouth shut and think before I speak.

Once I was at an HOBN meeting and a gentleman stood up to give his one-minute elevator speech. During his speech he asked if everyone would write a recommendation for him; if they had benefitted from advice he had given them. I blurted out, "Never ask for recommendations! We need to be pro-active and write recommendations for others first." I was thinking from my LinkedIn point of view, not regular recommendations. Why I blurted that out, I have no idea. It was a case of not thinking before I spoke. Someone in the group pointed that out to me and the very next week when I stood up to give my one-minute elevator speech, I first apologized to this gentleman. The way it came out, the group twisted it into a funny joke, but I think I got my apology across. It sure taught me a big lesson that I will remember for the rest of eternity.

Another realization I came to understand is that people have different comfort zones for how close you stand beside them.

I am a very huggie person and have a small radius around me for my comfort zone. From my experience, after going to hug someone and feeling them back away from me I realized that I needed to be aware of other people's space. I have a strong personality and some people are afraid of me because I come on a bit too strong. Little do they know that I love them all and just want to help them in any way I can. It has taken me some time to figure out how to be aware of comfort zones. It will always be a work in progress for me.

What is your comfort zone?

It can be as simple as shaking hands. When I was teaching a continuing education course at the Fraser Valley College back in 1990, the Director of the Small Business Development Department asked me to teach a course on how to market yourself and your business. We called the course, "Enhancing Your Personal Marketability". The first thing I did in the class was have all the students get up, go around the room shaking hands and introducing themselves. When they were all back in their seats, I asked them about the handshakes they had received. How did they feel? Did they receive a "limp fish" handshake? What about the "bone crusher" handshake? Or the "catch me if you can" handshake? Their reflections created an awareness they didn't have before the exercise.

I have worked on matching the grip with the person I am shaking hands with. It's kind of hard to do that when the person you are shaking hands with barely gives you their fingertips (catch me if you can). The way we shake hands has an impact on that first impression we are leaving with the person we are meeting. My challenge is to match the other person's grip and avoid squeezing too hard. As I used to milk cows by hand; therefore, my handshake is quite firm. As you can see we need to be conscious of everything we do, from shaking hands to thinking before we speak.

Have you found yourself in an embarrassing situation? How did you feel?

Every journey starts with learning. I have found the best way to learn is to keep an open mind and to never give up. Every person in this world has their own story to tell, I believe it is important to learn from others just as it is to allow others to learn from you. It's also important to accept another's background and culture as well. I believe this is accomplished by a continuous desire to want to learn new things.

I have also been a role model to others. Life isn't about ourselves; it's about what we can do for others. I believe it is a greater blessing to give than it is to receive and we can do this in many ways. First, I believe we have a responsibility to take care of those who are hurt and struggling; be it spiritually, mentally, emotionally, or physically. Second, to work with those less fortunate; and third, to use the gifts we have been given in life to benefit others.

The most important lesson I have learned in my life is to love and be loved. Should our acceptance of these differences be embraced and learned, how wonderful it would be and perhaps a more peaceful, loving world would be created.

It was at one of the HOBN meetings that I first met Joseph Eliezer. He is an "Intuition-Enhanced Psychotherapist" and an author. I was fascinated with how he expressed himself during his elevator speech and wanted to find out more about his work. I also wanted to see if there was a way we could work together. Since then, we have been working on a special workshop we could do together. Through my conversations with Joseph and his podcast interview, I have learned to be more attentive to listening to my deepest intuitions. In other words, as a result I listen to my "gut" more. I asked Joseph to write a contribution here as his advice looks at learning new tools like social media for your next step. Thank you, Joseph.

Finding you in an age of uncertainty

Right now, it's probably safe to say that your life doesn't look the way you want it to. You used to have a job or a career and now it's gone. You endured a loss. You're facing an enormous number of challenges and you don't want the career shift to be the financial end of you or the beginning of insignificance. Very likely, you are experiencing a wide range of emotions. Sometimes you feel overjoyed and super confident and at other times you experience fear, panic, and self-doubt.

Given what you're going through, let's address some of the feelings and struggles that are natural and understandable. It doesn't matter how much preparedness you've had, the loss of your status or position probably felt like a shock. At some point you likely felt helpless and you may have experienced fear, resentment, confusion, bitterness, insecurity, doubt, disconnectedness, abandonment, shame, and low self-esteem. Anger and confusion may be exacerbated by the fact that you lost your job at no fault of your own.

What do you do now?

Step 1. Acknowledge, feel, and express your feelings

In order to move forward and find yourself again, you must give yourself permission to feel and express your emotions. The loss of a job, to which our sense of identity is tightly attached, is enormous. Therefore, feeling your feelings around it is crucial. Clearing yourself of emotional debris not only promotes mental and physical health, but it also reconnects you to a sense of clarity and well-being; which you are going to need as you move back into the workforce. Talk to someone who supports you and perhaps consider seeing a counselor or psychotherapist as you move through this challenging time.

Step 2. Be aware of hindrances

Since you last looked for work it's likely the economy has become less friendly. Technology is also rapidly changing. As you try to re-establish yourself in the workplace, you may be up against many other candidates who are younger than you. The self-doubting voice in your head will inevitably try to derail you. "Who is going to hire me at this age? What am I good for? I can't compete with the youngsters. I will never recover from this." If you are faced with such self-messages, see them for they are: hindrances over which you have complete control. A simple recognition that negative thoughts are not helpful will free you of them. Once you acknowledge what isn't helpful, turn to what is helpful.

Step 3. Take stock of your skills and talents

Because of where you are in life (age-wise) you have acquired wisdom that is needed by others. You didn't get here by accident. You may not be in your twenties, but you have an entire roster of developed skills and talents that have worked for you before and will work for you again. Your ability to get things done in an expedient and swift manner; for example, is a skill that likely took several years to master. You know how to present yourself in a cohesive and mature manner (that took time too) and you understand the complexities of running a business day to day.

If you have trouble identifying what you are good at, ask those who know you well, whether former colleagues, friends or family. People generally like propping other people up and you may find you have many more allies than you realize. Your supporters might point out the strengths you haven't even thought of as marketable. If need be, consider taking a class to learn a new necessary skill or to refresh an old one. Sometimes, all it takes is to get recertified in your area of expertise. It doesn't matter what course of action you choose, above all, value your wisdom and experience that made you the strong, unique and self-aware person you are today.

Step 4. Network, network, network

It has been said before that it isn't what you know, or who you know, but who knows you. Employers still prefer tapping into their own social networks for a potential candidate rather than running ads that bring hundreds of applicants to sift through and interview. You need to be in that social network. The more people who know you're looking for a job, the better your chances are of finding one. Expansion of your social circle will be a necessary and on-going task. It involves a two-prong approach: (a) re-connecting with people who you already know and (b) networking to create new relationships with others.

Telling people in your already existing social network that you are looking for a job may feel awkward and even humiliating at first. As in Step 2, acknowledge these shameful feelings as hindrances and do what is helpful – connect. The more you do it, the less apprehensive you will feel. You might actually start enjoying it.

As you source your own connections, open yourself to as many new options and opportunities as possible. The next door you walk through may lead you to your new career. It can happen anywhere and anytime, and this is where things can become really exciting. Join networking groups, strike up conversations where appropriate, and shake as many hands as you possibly can.

As a person with a lot of life experience you already know what it takes to form meaningful connections. The fact is: networking is critical to your success of plugging back into the workforce.

Let's refresh what qualities and actions you will need to employ as you prepare yourself for your next great move.

Be Prepared

"Luck is what happens when preparation meets opportunity" is a cliché, but it is true. In your case, being prepared means knowing what to say about yourself in under a minute (Step 3 will help you accomplish it) and how to ask for what you need. To support you in this task, you will need to be equipped with some printed material; for example, a business or calling card so that your potential referral source can easily find you. Ideally, you would also have a website or a LinkedIn Profile. Consult a marketing specialist for ideas on how to make yourself visible in the modern world, driven by the social media. Get ready and wait for the opportunity to present itself. Then pounce.

Be Patient

Right now, your income is probably not skyrocketing and it's likely your situation isn't easy to tolerate. It doesn't matter how much nervous energy or worry you feel, refrain from making decisions from a place of insecurity. Hasty decisions, driven by anxiety, will most likely cost you more in the long run. Expecting immediate results might be unrealistic, so give yourself a fair amount of time for the fruits of your labour to start showing themselves.

Be Authentic

Connecting with others first and foremost requires authenticity. When you go to networking or other social functions, remember people want to do business and connect with those they like and trust. Represent yourself honestly, be transparent and be congruent with who you are as a human being and a professional. Sometimes we resort to subtle manipulation to get our needs met, but most of the time people sense our game and pull away. If you state your needs openly, you're more likely to make a good impression regardless whether the person in front you is able to meet your needs. By being authentic, you are building trust, and trust is the foundation of strong connections, which is your goal.

Be Present

At times, people you interact with will do and say things you won't like, appreciate or approve of. Your ability to recognize your own feelings and handle your own negative reactions productively and proactively will have an enormous impact on your ability to connect with others. If you aren't present to your emotions, you can't address them with yourself or the other person. If you aren't able to address what's bothering you, you will not be able to resolve potential conflicts and establish genuine connections. In addition, if you aren't present to your own process, you will miss the moment when your intuition whispers that something is off. Being connected to yourself and allowing yourself to feel what is unfolding at any given moment is being present. Acting appropriately on what you feel inside will improve the quality of your connections: you will avoid the destructive relationships and build on positive ones.

If you are uncomfortable feeling certain emotions or if your feelings are too intense for you to deal with on your own, let somebody (counselor, therapist, friend, associate) help you to develop your skill set. The ability to be present is an invaluable ally that will serve you well for the rest of your life.

Be Dependable

It is a simple tenet, but an important one: always deliver. As you shake hands with people and tell them about yourself, you might volunteer to find relevant information for them, send an email or facilitate a connection. Always follow through on every minute detail. If you promise to show up somewhere, make sure you do. As you expand your networking circles, your reputation will follow you. Being the person others can count on is a rare and admirable quality. Be that rare person.

Be Emotionally Generous

As you strive to make new connections and create a new life, it's important to remember that no one ever wants to wind up in the bin that Neal Diamond called forgotten. We all want to feel that we do matter and make a difference to people. In order to create memorable impressions with people, be willing to give of yourself. Wisdom shared by a person who is prepared, patient, authentic, present, dependable, and emotionally generous is extremely potent.

Give people your full attention as you listen to their stories. Find out how you can help them, and if you can, give of yourself fully and without expectation. Learn to look for the positive in people, and when you see it, let them know. Seeing others in a positive light helps them to feel better about themselves and increases their desire to have contact with you.

Give for the sake of giving: without any ulterior motive. Your emotional generosity will be remembered. You will be remembered, which is exactly what you are striving for when forming new connections and prospecting employers.

Last Words

Moving forward, however bad the circumstances may appear to be is of paramount importance. When you come upon situations that aren't a good fit, you are still in the process of movement, not stagnation. Movement is the place where you always want to be.

You're valuable. You're important. You're needed. There is a place for you. Anything is possible. Your challenge is to figure out where you best fit in this new, ever evolving paradigm. Although the paradigm might be new, what you are looking for is what everyone is looking for: it is something that feels meaningful and allows you to tap into your innate wisdom and develop connections with others. Finding something that makes you feel rested and energized simultaneously and that

reminds you that you are alive is the ultimate goal.
Joseph Eliezer
www.josepheliezer.com

Well, I needed to take Joseph's advice and put it into action. So, here I was getting deeper and deeper into social media and discovering the dos and don'ts of being on line and in real life. This is what I found through my discovery with social media and I would like to share it with you.

I use Sprout Social to set up all my posts.

I keep a record of all my posts (dates and times they are scheduled for) on a spreadsheet.

I make all my posts 140 characters (or less) including a shortened URL and they are compatible on all my platforms.

I schedule a minimum of four posts a day to all my platforms; for example, Twitter can be posted every couple of hours. Make sure what you are saying is relevant; for example, people don't want to know what you are having for lunch.

I create topics for my posts from my website, pod-blog, business, and experiences. In addition, I sometimes add a published article that is complimentary to my business.

I add my own special thought for the week, day and month; something original from me that I can use with a hash tag.

I only need to spend time organizing my postings once a month. I set up all my posts for the following month in advance.

I check my social media platforms for fifteen minutes a day to follow up on responses from people who want to connect with me.

I respond to each and every person who connects with me in all my social media, especially LinkedIn. I do this mostly through my Sprout Social platform.

I remember all those who I connect with are people too and I treat them with respect. I never, ever use four letter expletives in any of my posts, it doesn't matter how casual the conversation might seem to be with someone I know. You never know who might see it.

One of my learning curves was in discovering the uniqueness of the five basic social media platforms and it wasn't long before I noticed the way people were posting things on their Twitter, Facebook, and LinkedIn accounts.

YouTube is obvious, you post your videos on the site and then take the URLs and attach them to your other platforms. Google is a no-brainer. You need a profile on Google because it is the most powerful search engine on the Internet. If you have a profile on Google, it will find you wherever you are on the Internet.

I also signed up to receive Hub Spot's free social media information and e-zines. This is a great place to go for free on-line marketing information. They send out notices once a day that we can use with our businesses. I've discovered everything Hub Spot sends out is great and you really don't need to go anywhere else. It will save you massive amounts of time.

Sometimes I'm asked, "How should I respond to the people I meet in my social media? Can't I just be myself?" Yes, by all means, you must be somewhat transparent and be your genuine self.

There is a caveat, though.

When we are connecting on-line, we need to be even more careful of how we communicate and connect with people. The written word can be cold and can be easily misunderstood. People can't see your quirky smile as you type that comic remark; thus, it may not be taken in the light that you had intended. Remember to read everything you send as if you are the recipient before you send it - and double-check your spelling and grammar as well.

I have almost lost two great friendships because of misunderstood emails. I was being quip, but it came across as critical and hurtful. One was a dear friend whom I had worked with as my personal business coach. She has a habit of just plunging into the middle of her thoughts from the opening statement of her emails. They come across very strident and harsh. I don't think she realized it. One day she sent me an email that read, "Your attitude could use some straightening out! We need to talk…ASAP!" There wasn't a "Hi Christine" or "Happy Tuesday". There wasn't any greeting whatsoever. To just come out and say something like that was very hurtful and offensive. I felt I had been slapped in the face. I was stunned - to say the least. Now, I should have remembered that Abraham Lincoln handled this a lot differently. He would write a seething letter to express himself in response to someone and then place it in his desk drawer for a day or two before he sent it out. Do you know what happened? Old Abe never sent those letters. I let my feelings seethe and wrote a retort right back telling her that I was severing my relationship with her and any of her connections. To this day, I can't believe I did that. Her email caught me at a very stressful time in my life and it cut me to the core. It made me cry. The tears were streaming as I pounded the keyboard with my spicy retort. Thank goodness my dear friend went to a mutual friend and the two of them approached me in person. We kissed and made up and we are close friends to this day.

The second time this happened, it was I who was the original perpetrator. I sent an email to a very dear friend (whom I cherish to this day) and I had no idea my words had hurt her so deeply. She didn't tell me until we were both at a women's networking meeting where I was the speaker. Well, wouldn't you know it, I was speaking about on-line etiquette and how we needed to be more mindful of what we say and how we say it. Then I shared the above story. What happened next sent me reeling and stuttering in front of a whole group of women. My dear friend mentioned in a quiet tone that she had received an email from me that hurt her very deeply. She said that she sat and pondered what I had written for days; finally, she decided to ignore it. She was the wise one who practiced Old Abe's technique and we have remained dear friends to this day.

It has caused me to think about how many others out there

have misunderstood my written word and now I am very careful of what I say on-line.

Here are some tips on how to handle your different platforms of social media:

Twitter

This is the coffee shop chatter, the locker room chatter, and the photocopy room chatter. It needs to be authentic and make sense. Remember, no one wants to read what you had for lunch. This platform is the most interactive and you need to tweet on a regular basis. I have made some great connections and received some great help through this platform. A word of advice, remember the people who are tweeting to you are human beings and treat them that way.

Facebook

This is the company barbeque from a business point of view. You have a personal profile for your personal connections and can sort them into categories so your business contacts don't see your personal ones. However, if you have a business you need to have a business page. Once you have a business page you can invite people to "like" your page. Your business page should reflect your website.

LinkedIn

Now, this is my specialty. The reason I love this platform is because I have found some of my biggest clients from LinkedIn. This is the platform I use in order to first connect with key people who I want to invite as guests on my Marketing Mentress podcast show.

Why should you be using LinkedIn? Did you know that the average age of people on LinkedIn is 43? And the average annual income is $125K? There are over 150M people on LinkedIn and it's growing at a rate of one new sign up per minute? These statistics are only going to increase.

Now do you understand why you need to be using LinkedIn? Where do you think your target market is? Right, your target market is on LinkedIn. The people who can afford to buy your products and services are here. This is where the money is. This is where you can connect with your target market and bypass the gatekeepers. Have you ever tried to connect with a key decision maker by phone without first being introduced to them? Well, you can find these key people on LinkedIn, and connect with them directly: if you know how to work the platform.

Now even though we have all these social media tools, we still need to look at why we're doing all this. Do you know what Your "Why" is?

First, you need a big hook. What is your big hook? Do you have one? If you are wondering what a big hook is, it's your "Why" presented in such a fashion to feed someone else's need. When you are looking to make a connection on any of your social media, there are only so many polite emails you can exchange before you are asked about what you do. That is what you want; however, you need to be genuinely interested in the other person and ask them all about their business of what they do and why they do it. I like to find out what their "Why" is.

People will buy into you before they will ever buy into your what and how. Did you know that? Yet, what do we tend to do when we meet people at networking meetings? From my experience we tend to ask about the weather and what they do, but as soon as they ask us about what we do, we throw up all over them with how our product or service is so great and how it will help them and how they should use it, try it, or buy it. This is the reason I'm writing my book. I want people to know who I am and why I do what I do. Once they understand these things, it's my belief they will want to find out more about how they might be able to incorporate my services into their lives and businesses.

Chapter Four

Finding Your Why

Another workshop I was able to trade a podcast for was Colin Sprake's Business Mastery One. Colin is a master at presenting his workshops and my business did a "180" when I took his program. He has multiple programs, but the first one I feel everyone should take is this one on Business Mastery. The tools I learnt in his program changed how I did business - and my relationship with my husband forever. Without spilling the beans entirely, I will share a couple of little tidbits with you.

Colin helped me in two key areas. The first area was with my relationship with my husband. I used to get all upset when he was upset. I felt he got his knickers in a twist over little things. It caused huge stress in my life. On the first day, Colin shared with the group about "biting into someone else's apple". I thought to myself, "Who would want to do that?" The example he shared was about him and his wife. He said when he came through the front door, all in a froth and rattling on about something his wife would greet him, look at him, then turn and walk into another room. One day he asked her about her behaviour and she said, "I'm not biting into your apple." Do you know what? It works. I have since shared this tip with my husband and we both practice it with each other. Life at home is much less stressful now.

The second thing Colin taught me was how to find my "Why". At the end of the second day our assignment was to go home and write our story about what stood out in our lives from childhood. We were to write about our loves, concerns, regrets, hopes, dreams, and obstacles.

As I worked through my assignment, my "Why" jumped out at me. I realized my deepest desire was to help other people who found themselves in the same position as myself: five to 15 years short of their financial goals and over 50. My heart wanted to teach them how to dig deep into their tool chest and find the tools they could offer society and monetize themselves. I wanted to help them learn how to navigate social media and keep it simple.

When I got involved with social media, it was all at once. I set up my profiles on all the basic platforms in one evening. I was ploughing through the Internet trying to absorb it all at once. I wanted to show people that there is a simple way to master this tsunami and manage it: instead of it managing you. I wanted to help them attain clients and make sales so they could have a decent lifestyle in the coming years.

When I was first learning about the key platforms, I had five different platforms running through my head all at one time. I felt my head was going to burst at any moment. The frustration was stupendous. The tears were many.

Colin's program helped me to sort out my "Why" and why I'm so driven to coach LinkedIn and social media to help my brothers and sisters through their social media challenges. I can't thank Colin Sprake (www.makeyourmark.com) enough for what his workshop did for me. I will help him market his programs forever.

Now that I had all my social media platforms set up and was going to networking events my next learning curve was to speak to people I didn't know. Here's a technique I learnt from Dale Carnegie about how to converse with people. When I went to meetings I would hang back in the crowd. After the initial "Hello" I wouldn't know what to say. As soon as people would ask about me, I would start talking about myself and never shut up. I was stuck in the "me" mode and didn't know how to get out of it.

Years before, when I was working as a business consultant with the Fraser Valley College in their Business Owner Development Program, the director invited me to attend the Dale Carnegie course to help me with my name recall and public presentation. The course was starting the following week and the organizer had offered the college one free ticket. The director had already taken the course a few years earlier; thus, the ticket was mine if I wanted it. I am so grateful for that opportunity. I learnt so much about how to listen to people, how to get them talking about themselves, and about how to remember their names.

Did you know that a simple F-O-R-M is the key to all conversations? F-family; O-occupation; R-recreation; M-message. Everyone loves to talk about their family, their occupation and what they like to do when they aren't at work. As you ask questions concerning F-O-R, you can listen to the responses and steer the questions you ask to the point where you will find out if they are looking for help. You might choose not to give them your message because of their responses to the first F-O-R. When I can see they're not interested in what I have to offer, I will lightly ask for a referral instead. The key thing to remember is never to "pitch your stuff" at the first meeting.

A soft approach works miracles. All I do now is invite. It's a numbers game, in other words I'm planting seeds. Not every seed will sprout, but you want to leave the most positive impression possible with everyone you meet. It doesn't matter who they are. What kind of an impression are you leaving with the people you meet?

How to make a Great First Impression.

You have less than three seconds to make a great first impression. I am reminded of a wealthy farmer from my life in Red Deer, Alberta. He was our neighbour. This farmer was a hard worker and never walked around dressed in anything other than his overalls usually with one strap hanging down his back. He always wore a plaid, flannel shirt and long underwear. This outfit was topped off with his work boots with the laces undone part way down. He did look a sight.

He banked at a local major bank, and had done so for many years. One day he went into his bank dressed as he always did, and speaking gruffly, as he always did, to do his regular banking. Well on that fine day there was a new teller serving him and this young lady didn't know him. When he gave her a check for a large sum of money and asked to have it cashed: she panicked.

In those days there weren't any computers. Transactions were handled by check or cash and credit cards were rare. Well, this young lady took one look at this vagabond and thought he was trying to rob the bank. She spoke abruptly to our farmer friend telling him that she would have to first get his check approved. Little did she know that this particular scruffy looking farmer was a multi-millionaire and had all his money in this bank. The farmer was insulted to his limits. He then asked to speak to the manager and requested a withdrawal of all his money from the bank. He took his money and went across the street to the competition and set up his accounts there; thus, leaving that manager and his teller standing in shock.

I would agree that our farmer friend could have been more aware of his appearance and put forth a more concerted effort to create positive first impressions when he was out and about. Was it the teller's fault that she judged him based on her first impression? Can you see how this would have completely changed the story, if he had?

Let me share another story from when I was working as a legal secretary. There were two gentlemen in competition for an accounting position. They both arrived dressed in freshly pressed suits, ties, crisp white shirts, and black shoes. They both had similar credentials. They were both clean-looking with short haircuts and were clean-shaven. Concurrently, they both seemed to take care of details when their references were checked.

Well, the Director of Human Resources was at a stalemate and didn't know whom to pick, so she invited them each to join her for lunch - on different dates of course. During the meal, she watched their manners and how they conducted themselves at the table. The HR director also noted their impeccable dress, including their shoes and socks. After lunch each candidate was thanked politely for coming with the appropriate thank you letter.

However, it was during lunch that one of the young prospects cinched the position! The HR Director noticed that one young man didn't have his shoes polished and he had terrible table manners. This display wasn't one that the company wanted their clients to witness. So, guess who got the job? Yes, it was the young man with the impeccable grooming, suit, tie, shirt, clean shaved face, polished shoes, and good table manners.

It was at an HOBN meeting that I met Mick Lolekonda. One morning, as I sat in my chair at the huge table, in walked a tall, striking and well put together young man with a beautiful smile. He had such a great way of making everyone feel at ease around him. Plus, by the way he conducted himself and spoke, I knew he was educated and that he was speaking from personal experience. We became good friends and Mick has filmed my full day workshop on LinkedIn to capture the material I needed for my new website. He is a very talented young man! I asked Mick Lolekonda for his advice as he has been a great example through his actions, words, and how he treats people. Mick dresses sharp, is always neatly dressed. Mick has mastered the three-second first impression. This is the advice he gives.

But first, who is Mick? He is originally from the Democratic Republic of Congo and has lived in Western Europe, Northern Africa, the United States and now Canada. In 2002, during Mick's College years, the entrepreneurial flame was ignited in him. At that time he decided to go into business for himself. After finishing school in 2003, his journey led him (after mostly having sales positions with Fortune 100 companies) to start his first solo-business in 2008: a dating and relationship business. Being responsible for all aspects of his coaching business, this hands-on business experience better prepared him for his latest launched venture in 2011: Red Sneakers Mediaworks. His company's mission is to help clients attain visibility through video marketing. Mick believes there are individuals with talents, gifts and expertise driven to make a difference; therefore, their communities need to know their businesses exist.

Thank you, Mick!

Insights for someone in their 50s, unemployed and 5-15 years short of their financial goals. By Mick Lolekonda

As you are now unemployed, all you have left is your ability to make money for yourself. You are now in business for "You Inc" and it's time to get to work because there isn't any time to waste. Why? Because from now on, time is your most precious commodity. The rules are now simple: If you don't find clients, you don't get paid; if you don't get paid, you can't put food on the table and have a roof over your head.

The corporate world can see you as an expensive liability, whereas the world and the people you are meant to lead or serve see your life experience as an invaluable source of knowledge to draw from. They realize with your help they can improve their lives, businesses, health, and even raise their spirits. And what a great position to be in: one where you make a difference in someone's life.

So look at this as the best opportunity of your life because it's your time to shine. You are now in a privileged position where it is one hundred percent up to you to decide what you are going to do considering these unforeseen circumstances. Are you going to fight or fold?

This is a question I ask myself every time I want to

remind myself that I'm in control of my destiny. Your attitude will help you get through this and your ability to stay positive and willingness to learn, or relearn, key skills. Based on my experience, the following steps are a few suggestions now that you are on your own.

Make a list of all the things you are naturally good at, those that bring you joy every time you do them. These are your strengths, the things you love doing and leave you feeling energized once you've finished doing the work. Personally, I love consulting with clients, and creating a marketing needs analysis of their business and life situation as it leads to offering them a custom solution. This is what gets me going.

Now, what gets you going? As an exercise, create a list of what you love doing as part of your work. You'll see as your "You Inc." grows, this list will remind you what tasks need to be delegated or outsourced. Those tasks are the ones that aren't your strengths and others can do the job better and faster than you. If you don't do this, these particular tasks will eat away at your time, taking you away from moneymaking activities.

Since we are on the topic of money-making activities, I suggest you start thinking in terms of your value. How much are you worth an hour? Once you determine that, do your best to not do anything that costs less than your value per hour. For example, let's service a client (from the consultation to getting the sale and doing the actual work) and it takes a total of 5.5 hours at $500.00 per package: your value is about $91.00/hour.

Knowing that, avoid doing tasks within your business that pay less than $91.00/hour. Doing so will put your business on the fast track to be a thriving business. Remember your role is to focus on what you do best and delegate the rest unless you want to do it all yourself.

Of course, as you start, you may have to do everything and that's okay. As your business evolves, find ways to delegate those tasks by contracting them out. As a side-note, I don't suggest hiring employees when starting, I believe in contracting the right talent.

The next thing to think of is verbalizing your "Why". In other words, your reason for doing what you do. Your "Why" is the magnet that will create a following of individuals who will buy from you because they can relate to your "Why". Remember: the "Why" creates communities. Whenever people ask what it is you do, always find a way to sneak in your "Why" into the conversation. Believe me, it'll make all the difference. To see what I mean, check out the welcome video on www.redsneakersmediaworks.com. If you're wondering how to create your "Why", I suggest going over your past life experiences, challenges, the lessons learnt and ponder: "How and why can this help someone who used to be in my shoes?" And based on the answers you get, craft your "Why" and message around the feedback you receive.

Once you're ready to launch "You Inc." take the first six months to tell people what you are doing and why. Treat it as an experiment. You're the business scientist taking in all feedback. Start today with what you have and allow the market to tell you whether you are on the right track or not. Adopting this strategy of testing the market by surveying people, joining associations, speaking to groups, getting one client at a time will provide you with valuable market research data. Data that you can; for example, use to adjust your pricing, fine-tune your service packages, realize when you need extra people on your team and so much more. It'll only happen once you take action and meet new people: staying at home won't help you.

By now you've been working on your business and focusing on getting new clients. At this point you should be cash-flow-focused and will have determined how you will sustain yourself. Even if you do have savings to help you cruise for a while, I strongly suggest acting as if you're broke.

Be aware of what your living expenses add up to. If you need to downgrade your lifestyle, now is the time to do it. Determine your living expenses and my rule of thumb is two clients should help cover your living expenses. As you develop your business, strive to change these parameters into having one client equal one-month living expenses. You would do so by increasing prices over time or create a new package with a higher price tag.

As you start to get clients and money starts flowing in, my suggestion is to predetermine how you'll manage that money. It is imperative that you develop the know-how to keep your money, budget properly, and not live pay-check to pay-check. This has probably been the biggest lesson I learnt as an entrepreneur. So to help with this, I suggest talking to an accountant or a financial planner before you start making money.

Learn or re-learn fundamental sales skills that include knowing how to find the right prospects, to sell them, and get referrals. For this I recommend getting your hands on a business classic, "The psychology of Selling" by Brian Tracy. Another great book to consider is: "Book Yourself Solid" by Michael Port.

Leap into this new adventure because you have no other choice. And rest assured, as you spend more time working on your business, meeting people, getting clients, making adjustments, your business will evolve. Your pricing will evolve as well as your business savvy and acumen.

At this point you make believe your business goal should be to get as many clients as possible. I don't recommend it, instead allow your business to grow organically, just as a plant does. Focus and strive to improve your processes and bettering your clients' experience before getting an avalanche of them.

Know that you'll drop the ball and make mistakes. I know I have, but it's part of the learning process. I've priced packages too low and I ended up not making any money, I've had clients who ended up with a poor experience and as a result I had to issue refunds. It happens, just remember not to be hard on yourself. Take the time to improve your processes and make the necessary adjustments before looking to hit the masses with your services.

Also keep in mind that not every client is the right one for you. Sometimes you'll have to say "no" to a potential client and it's okay to do so. Sometimes you'll have to refund an unhappy client; some clients will drain you and make your life difficult. When you feel that you aren't able to provide the best service, refer them to someone who can be a better fit for them.

When it comes to revenue, look at year one as the seeding year, the year where you won't make any money. You'll make some money, but not a full-time income, so plan to have another source of revenue as you build "You Inc." During this year, be determined meet a lot of the right people who will either become clients, strategic partners or referral sources.

Year two is when you start reaping what you sowed. You're getting more referrals; people in your community now know you and your brand; your processes have been fine-tuned as year two is the break-even year.

Year three is where you should determine whether it makes sense for you to stick it out or find another business avenue. You may find something is missing and there could be a better opportunity for you in a different venture, which is okay. The questions to ask yourself are: Is that fire in your belly still there when you look at your business? How do you feel after working with clients? Does it feel effortless? And how about the money, does it come easily? Those questions should help you determine where you stand.

And if you're one of the lucky ones whose business gets off the ground like a rocket within those two years, congratulations.

Now, being unemployed doesn't necessarily mean you have to start a business. There are other paths where your life and work experience will be highly valued. Many sales organizations look for the right independent agents to represent their already established brand. If you have an entrepreneurial spirit, this is a great way to still utilize it without the challenges a business owner faces.

A great example of this is financial institutions, especially those specializing in financial planning. Could this be the right path for you? Now is the perfect time to assess all your possibilities.

Another thing to consider is the fact that we live in a technology and information-driven society. Thanks to the Internet, the world now has access to you and vice versa. If the idea of having to deal with technology is intimidating, I can see why you may feel that way. However, if you believe that you can learn anything and I know you can, there are some basic things that you can learn to feel comfortable on the Internet as well as marketing yourself online. And if this doesn't appeal to you, remember you can reach out to someone who's more knowledgeable in this area than you are. Look for marketing or online marketing consultants in your area. They usually belong to associations and can also be found online.

Nowadays, it's easy to find the right connections you need and even prospects online through social media platforms. If you're not familiar with those platforms, there are online communities where people who share something in common, congregate. By the way, the popular social media sites include: Facebook, LinkedIn, Twitter, and Google+.

Learn how to find those connections and prospects and you can fast track your ability to make more money early on in your new business career. And there are a variety of trainers out there, including The Marketing

Mentress, who can help you in that department better than I can.

If you find yourself in a position where you wonder what industry to operate your business in, know that there's no need to reinvent the wheel - unless you want to. To this effect, I suggest looking for industries where people are already spending their money. The relationship industry is a good example because you can tell by the amount of books that have been written on the subject. The same thing applies with topics relating to personal development or sales and management.

Generally speaking, one can choose various business avenues to operate in including business and money, relationships, spirituality, health. When choosing a business avenue, determine which one applies to you best incorporates most of your natural interests and passion. Make the best decision with the understanding that you might change avenues later. You may start working the relationship avenue and things may go okay. But then, because you realize that you really like business, you may end up switching avenues to the business and money avenue. All of sudden, it's easier to get clients, raise your prices, and you feel things are happening effortlessly.

To help choose the right avenue, think, why do people usually ask you for help? Is it about a business matter, their career, relationship or health issues? What do people say you're good at? If you're unsure, simply ask the people who really know you. They'll tell you.

You may find after choosing one avenue, you realize that you are better suited for another. It can happen and it's okay. When you find yourself in this position I would advise you to not be attached to the idea of what your business means to you and your ego. Those things include (but are not limited to): social status, the cool factor and even good money. Nothing replaces fulfillment and you may need to be courageous and even bold enough to let go of the old business and the old identity that was attached to it. I say this because I experienced this personally.

What you'll most likely find on the other side is fulfillment and possibly even more financial success: be open to changing and evolving.

As I bring my contribution to this book to an end, I'd like to hit on four points. First, whatever industry and line of work you choose, others most likely have already paved the way for you. So learn from the best. Find mentors, advisors, and even coaches who will help you get on the right path. Their knowledge can be accessible in person, but also on books and audiotapes or CDs.

Second, take care of your health because your success depends on your ability to get out there. I suggest that you create a health and fitness plan. If you are over 50, you can easily search online for an exercise program for over 50 or an exercise program for women over 50.

Third, if you find yourself 5 to 15 years short of your financial goals around when you're around 50 years old, don't despair, you have time. According to the World Bank, the life expectancy in North America is around 78.5 years old for men and 83 for women. This being said, I strongly suggest having on paper what financial target you must hit ten years from now. How much income will you need to live on once you decide to retire on your own terms? Of course, get yourself the right financial planner and business advisor who will help you come up with a clear plan and stick to it.

Fourth, go where the money is. It is possible to do all the right things in the wrong places. If you network or market yourself in areas where prospects haven't the money to invest in your services or companies haven't a budget for your services, your business will suffer, you'll get frustrated and even think of quitting.

I wish all the blessings, happiness, and success you

deserve. I know you'll do great because the world has been waiting for you all along.

Thank you Christine, The Marketing Mentress for inviting me to be a part of your book. I am touched and humbled.

Mick Lolekonda

www.redsneakersmediaworks.com

Well, after taking in everyone's advice you can pool all your tools together and find your own tool chest and figure out how to move forward. I realize most of you reading these words probably don't have a modicum such as podcasting or a book that you can trade for help: but think hard. I'm sure there is something you are great at, something to give value to people, something they would be willing to trade for.

Are you a great writer or efficient typist? Do you know how to spell and edit documents? If you are a writer, perhaps you can turn your skills to writing blogs, articles and help other people to write. As a coach, you could get qualified and teach English as a Second Language (ESL). If you are a great cook, you could put together your best recipes and publish your own special recipe book. Perhaps you're a bookkeeper, you could start a small accounting business from your home. As an artist, you could loan out your artwork for display on a monthly rental basis to businesses and condominium complexes. What I'm suggesting is: You could take any trade and make a business out of it.

I'd like to share a story. My accountant mentioned to me that he had a fellow who came around every few months to wash his office windows and he never thought anything of it. It wasn't expensive, so he just paid cash every time. Well, at the end of the year, this window washer came to my accountant and asked him to file his taxes for him. This window washer made close to $125K that year. You can imagine my accountant's surprise.

Gardening is another physical occupation. If the property

owner can't do it, he needs someone else to do it for him. According to my accountant, gardening companies make great money. He would never share any numbers with me, but it's well over $100K annually.

I have discovered there are many people and services available out there to help us for free. There are university students who are studying marketing and they need to work on projects in order to complete their credits. They'll help you with power point presentations, website development, design logs: They can even help with writing and assembling workbooks for your workshops.

Check out local business schools and colleges to tap into the business students available for free help and coaching while setting up your business. Think about CGA students and CA students as well. If these students want to be paid, it will be little compared to paying a fully trained accountant or business coach. We must be careful not to exploit these students, however.

Whatever you do (to get yourself into a position where you can monetize yourself) please remember that you will save yourself a lot of time and money if you will just ask for help and take every advantage you can for professional assistance with your business.

As 2011 progressed, I became more adept with social media: especially LinkedIn. Plus, all the podcasts and posting them through my social media platforms gave me a wonderful gift: The gift of knowledge and expertise in managing social media efficiently and timely.

It also gave me the gift of a greater love of people along with a huge desire to help my fellow human beings in business. How are you feeling about your strengths and talents at this moment? Do you know what yours are?

The arrows in my quiver are: public speaker, singer, performer, educator, podcaster, and an avid learner. I sat down with a sheet of paper and wrote down all my strengths on one side and on the other side I wrote down exactly how I could use these strengths.

I also noted how I could use each strength to trade for services I needed in order to build my self-esteem and my business.

After my experience, I suggest that you use your strengths to get the help you need to decide how to package yourself into a marketable commodity. Remember, you can't do it alone. It will take you twice as long to achieve success if you insist on being a lone wolf. Believe me, we all need help getting started with our businesses.

One of the great interviews I had the privilege of conducting on my podcast show was with Dwayne Klassen from "The Remarkable Man Project". He is brilliant and shared his story of how he transformed himself after losing everything he held dear to him in his life. We had a private LinkedIn coaching session afterward, and he mentioned that he had a dear friend who wanted to take advantage of my LinkedIn coaching. That is how I met Laura Simonson. We have completed two podcast interviews on my show. Laura has developed a top quality and totally vegan dog food. As you read her comments you will understand her wisdom and how amazing she is! To end this chapter I invited Laura Simonson to add her thoughts here about how she pulled her strengths together to become "The Doggess."

Thank you, Laura!

Peace sister, *fear* not, your life is just beginning…

I am Laura Simonson, passionate businesswoman and relentless entrepreneur. My handle is, The Doggess -- a peace-lovin', 50 year old woman embarking on an extraordinary adventure to release the hounds on outdated perceptions of a vegetarian lifestyle with one aim: to inspire all women, men, and their dogs to give the New Veg and peace a chance.

I am determined to take every mind, body, spirit seeking goddess sister and brave brother for the joy ride of their lives. How am I going to do this? By launching my life dream: a vegetarian food, services, and events brand, with a lofty, scary goal to put a loving dent in the universe. So, why did I self-proclaim myself, The Doggess? Well, it is a "Dogma to Doggess" novel in the making; however, these words are to hopefully inspire you on your search to find, You.

Here's the skinny. First, if you are reading this, I am assuming you have arrived at one of the most important intersections of your life. You have a fire in your belly, a dream that is yearning and churning deep in your soul and you know with all of your heart it could be a viable business or perfect career change, but you are scared. Yup, scared. You are filled with fear, anxiety, paranoia, terror, fright, catastrophic nightmares, dread, panic and wondering if there is something deeply wrong with you. Why can't you just tell your husband, your partner, your best friend, your mother, your co-worker, your dog that what you *really, really, really* want to accomplish with your life is through a business or entirely new career? Well that question could have many answers, but at some level, the answer is fear. One of my favourite quotes that keeps me sane and gets me through my immense fear is by Jules Feiffer, he confesses, "I told the doctor I was anxiety ridden, compulsively active, constantly depressed, with recurring fits of paranoia. Turns out I'm normal."

Yes, you are normal. So, if you are deciding at this moment, and as you are entering into what Jane Fonda calls our, "Third Act" of life, to begin anew - run - don't walk and make this *normal* fear, your best friend. Let fear be the amplifier behind your passion as you prepare to shout your dream from the rooftop of your condo, suburbia home, and office tower or yoga studio.

It took me close to 50 years to figure out fear is normal and in fact, is the *human* part of our "human being". In my past, fear was actually a profound motivator for me to begin businesses or walk with my head high after being asked abruptly to leave a job. I couldn't have articulated it this way before, but fear assisted me to become better at sports, better at school, better at work, better at being fired, better at relationships, and better at launching a business. The key for me was to finally admit: I am scared. But now, it is a teeny tiny voice versus an excruciating scream inside my head. Now, my "soul" has the final say; however, it certainly hasn't always been that way.

I was born in a small town, on the other side of the tracks, a prairie girl of mixed, colorful heritage: Ukrainian and Norwegian. My childhood and teenage years were both brutal and blissful. During the lonely, brutal times, my dogs, food and God were my trusted friends. They all listened to my fears and my dreams. You see, fear was imbedded so deep within my siblings and me, sometimes it's a wonder we survived those crazy and anguish-filled days. From Bab, my live-in Ukrainian grandmother describing her dreaded days during the Russian revolution and Great Depression to my father's emotional and physical abuse, it is another wonder I am able to write these words.

Now, fast-forward to 1987 when I woke up. I began to recognize I was robbed. Yes, by others, but most important: by myself. I discovered this by gleaning the wisdom of thought leaders and goddesses such as: Louise Hay, Shirley MacLaine and Marianne Williamson to name a few. I realized I was a victim of fear and that year I chose to dive into personal growth and awareness.

I discovered my fears had turned into obsessions such as sports, food, and unhealthy relationships. They weren't just cultural or for distraction, they were actually a link to my healing and to forgiving. They were also a powerful link to me *discovering my purpose*. Although incredibly counter-intuitive, the fears actually inspired me to begin all of the businesses that were conceived

through my passions, which have led me to today and
to the launch, my most amazing dream.

My big dream was birthed during the late 80's. I
was divinely led to read John Robbin's revolutionary
book (at that time) "Diet for a New America". John's
profound words shared the intimate details of factory
farming and inhumane acts subjected to animals. The
facts caused a paradigm shift within me and I began my
journey of being a vegetarian.

Years later, a few days after the tragedy of Sept 11,
2001, I was inspired (through love and fear!) to seek out
the border collie I had always wanted. I even had her
name chosen: Shanti which means peace in Sanskrit. I
had also researched and planned her vegetarian diet.
That was over ten years ago now.

Shanti came into my life at a time when the healing
path wasn't just rocky, it was filled with major boulders.
I was about to lose a business. And worse yet, lose my
reputation as a health studio owner, personal trainer,
and international health and fitness coach. During the
next several years Shanti would be my confidant, my
companion, my running buddy and most important,
my sage. She sat with me every morning in meditation
as I healed, prayed, cried, dreamed, and as I made fear
my other best friend.

I have come to realize that in my early days, when
dogs, food and God were my trusted friends, they were
like a premonition. It's as though this gig and having
Shanti in my life were divinely planned. It's as though
the fear allowed me to truly, truly embrace my purpose,
which in turn caused me to get Shanti. From my
experience with her, I'm launching a vegetarian food
company for dogs, people, and our planet from my
passion to share, love, and inspire.

Then, just like a true fairy tale and by staying true to
my purpose, I met him: Gord. He entered my life when
I allowed myself to be vulnerable and scared. He is now

my true love, my business partner, my best friend, and my mentor. He is supporting me in every way possible for my big dream to come true and to embrace the fear.

Fear was my guide to goodness. Fear was the dogma in order for me to embrace my "Doggess". Yes, I am sometimes neurotic, paranoid, and anxious, but now I understand that if I just "sit", like Shanti and allow myself to just "be", I will get the answer through the fear, since I now know is just my friend.

A question I often asked myself that I learnt from a friend, extraordinary man and coach, Davender Gupta, "Is what you're doing right now creating the future you want?" If the answer is "No", then fear is simply asking you to consider it as part of your decision to do something that will create the future you want.

Lastly, please remember, fear is courage in disguise and if you are feeling scared right at this minute, feel it, love it, and embrace it. You are normal and you will realize your dream. Believe it.

Peace sister, *fear* not, your life and business are just beginning.

Laura Simonson, Founder, Indogo Life and The Doggess www.indogolife.com and www.doggess.com

There are also business and life coaches of all categories that you can access for free. Check out Betska K-Burr's company. She trains people to be Business and Life Coaches. These trainees need to do some volunteer coaching in order to qualify for their graduation as professional coaches. In other words, they need to log practical time to complete their certification. Now here is an offer you cannot refuse!

Business and Life Coaching Creates Miracles

From Betska K-Burr, Accredited Master Coach (IIC), best-selling author.

I was fired at the age of 37! Every writer in this chapter knows that picking ourselves up after the fall is not easy unless we have a Business and Life Coach. Laura, for example, mentioned 'fears'. Emotions such as doubt, lack of faith in self and so on are all common whether we are fired at 37, 50 or 65! The pain can be excruciating.

Today, as a Master Coach and someone who trains Business and Life Coaches around the world, I know without a shadow of a doubt that if you wish to be successful in business and in life THE most important things you must get rid of are your fears and negative thoughts/judgments about yourself and others. Why? Because those fears and emotions stop us in our tracks – they stop us from moving forward. Remember the Universal Law 'What we think we become'? If we have a fear, we will attract that fear. If we deeply connect with a goal, we will attract that goal.

Referencing the new science by Bruce Lipton, Candace Pert and some lady named Betska K-Burr (he he), we know that when we can't achieve a goal or overcome a challenge it is simply because the receptors sitting on the cell membrane in charge of that thought are constricted. Food and nourishment cannot enter the cell and thus underfed cells cannot think clearly.

It is that simple.

Also vitally important to recognize is that fact that if we don't get rid of our fears and unconstructive emotions, this dis-ease could become disease.

A well trained Business and Life Coach must be able to:

- Help you discover the root cause of the fears and emotions stopping the energy and food from entering the cell;
- Discover your unconstructive beliefs about yourself and others at a subconscious level because the subconscious mind is the storehouse

of all of our beliefs and is one million times more powerful than our conscious mind;

- Replace those negative beliefs with permanent positive ones and only then can we move forward. We affectionately call this 'popping of receptors'.

Only then, with fears and emotions out of the way, you can see more clearly and achieve your goals and dreams.

CLI is an all Canadian company with Coaches from across the globe studying with us to become brilliant Coaches. To access students who can do the work for free and/or access very highly trained PCMK Coaches visit www.Coachingandleadership.com and then click on "Choose a Coach". You may also wish to self-coach using these amazing free-of-charge self-coaching tools at www.TheBrainWalk.com.

May God bless your path and keep you peaceful and joyful.

Betska K-Burr is an Accredited Master Coach (IIC). Her Clients and students affectionately call her The Guru Coach™.

Some key books I highly recommend to read are:

- "The "God" in Coaching – The Key to a Happy Life" by Betska K-Burr
- "How to Win Friends and Influence People" by Dale Carnegie
- "Think and Grow Rich" by Napoleon Hill.
- "Developing the Leader within You" and "Developing the Leaders Around You" by John Maxwell

Chapter Five

Fake It Till You Make It

Now, how was I going to get exposed to the world? How was I going to get my podcasting services out into the marketplace? And how was I going to promote my services in a way that added value to people's businesses?

Essentially, what you have to do is "Fake It Till You Make It". When you go to networking meetings: dress sharp, put on your best smile, rise to your best positive attitude, and speak as though you have already attained your goal. You need to act and sound like you know what you are talking about. My question to you is, "Are you sold on you?" If you're not, everyone in those networking groups will know it the moment you enter the room. My advice: remember the three-second rule.

When you stand up to speak about your business, speak with confidence and have eye contact with every person sitting around the table. Have your elevator speech memorized so it rolls off your tongue smoothly and sounds like you have been doing it for years. If you don't know how to write an elevator speech, check out "Three Steps to a Great Elevator Speech" by Guy R. Powell. Once you have written your elevator speech, practice, practice, and practice. Stand in front of your bathroom mirror, your dog, your cat, and your stuffed teddy, whomever you can. Personally, I have done most of my rehearsing in front of the bathroom mirror and be aware of your body language, stand up straight, shoulders back. Have confidence when you walk in the room. Your entrance should be such that people feel your presence immediately and turn to see who is there. It's like being on a stage and you're about to give the performance of your life. Once you do it enough times, it becomes easy. That's faking it according to Christine.

It had been a while since I had done any networking; therefore, just getting back into the habit of physically getting myself out the door was a challenge. How was I going to introduce myself to people at these meetings? How was I going to show up looking larger than life and leave the lasting impression people would want to remember? What should I wear? How should I behave? How should I speak? My instinct was to stay at home in my little office and putter on my computer all day and night with my social media searching on-line for solutions to my marketing dilemma; however, I had to get out the door and meet people.

Earlier in the year, when I was first fired, I met with the Capilano University Small Business Development Department. When they heard the fee I was charging for my podcasting services they asked, "And what were you planning to do for that $250?" I explained my process (as you have read in the previous chapter) and they continued, "And you are charging how much for this service?" Again I said, "$250." Again they said, "And you are asking people to pay how much for this service?" By the third time I felt a little embarrassed and guessed that I was going to have to rethink what I was charging as it was clear I was asking far too little.

I walked out of the meeting and doubled my rates, from $250 to $497 per show.

Do you know what? That meeting at Capilano University had enormous value for me, because I used that knowledge on one of my shows. As I mentioned earlier, every person who has been a guest on my show has been my personal coach. I was able to use the gift of a podcast to trade for services and my education. It also gave me credibility.

From that point when I walked into a meeting and people asked me what I did, I told them that I had a podcast show. Well, everyone wanted to know what my show and me were about. Then, I would ask them about their work and what inspired them to start their business. I acted with all the confidence in the world, but I was dying inside for fear that people might see I'm a fraud and not what I professed to be. I realized that I had to be authentic at the same time: faking it was all about gaining the self-confidence. I needed to stand up in front of people and give my professional and confident elevator speech.

Another key tool I had in my toolbox was the training and knowledge about marketing myself as a person. As I attended many networking meetings, I watched business owners and took notes. I noticed those who were great at communicating their businesses and those who needed help with their pitch. From what I have witnessed, the two key things that stood out to differentiate the great from the mediocre: their appearance and their enthusiasm.

Enthusiasm on Fire Sells Far More Than Knowledge on Ice

If you want people to be sold on your business, first they need to be sold on you. Therefore, you need to know how to sell yourself. People buy into you and your "Why" long before they buy into your "How and What". My advice is this, be proud to share why you're in business; what is in your heart; what your passions are; and why you're doing what you do. People love that. Do you have your elevator speech prepared? Will you be believable when you stand up in a meeting and speak about your business?

While I was attending networking meetings, I had to appear like a duck. You know, calm on the surface and paddling like crazy underneath. What were the other tools in my toolbox? When I spoke, I listed my experience, training, and expertise. I was a polished public speaker. I was a classically trained vocalist and was loved by the seniors when I performed the old tunes for them. I was also an expert at doing cash flow projections and I was a good teacher. I had taught several different courses in conjunction with the Fraser Valley College in their Business Owner Development Program; however, that was old school teaching before the days of social media and the Internet.

The question was, of all these tools in my toolbox, which ones could I monetize? In other words, what could I offer to the world that had value in today's marketplace and one that people would pay for? What was my special niche in the market place that only I could fill? That was the big question. Then came the epiphany: voila!

I could teach workshops on LinkedIn. Now, I need to interject here for a bit. While I was attending these networking meetings, I noticed that sixty to seventy percent of the people sitting around those tables had grey hair. They were all in the same position as me. As I watched them stand up to give their elevator speech (they were people with bachelors, masters and doctorates degrees) they made their one minute speech into five minutes; throwing everything they could do at their audience with the hope that someone would buy what they were selling.

From my own personal life experience (as in the example above) combined with what I have witnessed I decided to write my book. This way I could use my book as my platform; people could use it as a self-help masterpiece for their own lives.

My experience using LinkedIn as a platform became so natural that I was using it on a daily basis to find people to be guests on my show. I soon realized I knew more than most people about LinkedIn. Today LinkedIn is the biggest arrow in my quiver. Yes I was getting some singing gigs for seniors groups, but they weren't paying a whole lot. At the rates I was being offered, I would have to be doing at least two gigs every day, seven days a week, in order to make a mediocre living. So, how was I going to market my expertise with LinkedIn?

To date, I had been working with businesses that had big-ticket items and from my podcasting they were starting to show some success. By December 2011: people were starting to pay for my services. The challenge was that most small businesses couldn't afford me at $1000 a month, plus another $500 per lead. As I attended networking meetings I saw many small businesses that were looking for customers. After all, why do people attend networking meetings? I met many people who were in similar situations to myself: a little grey hair at their temples, out of work, without any prospects. My heart went out to these people and I wanted to help them to be successful with their businesses. I knew I had a way to help them.

Upon watching the analytics of my social media through Sprout Social, I could see my followers were 60% male and 40% female, on average. I wondered, why? I discovered men are more focused on one thing at a time and will take time to stick to a task until they figure it out. Women, on the other hand, always have multiple balls in the air. When they first try LinkedIn, they see it is complicated and say, "I don't have time for this." Then they promptly leave it until another day. Well, another day never comes to most women, because they see themselves as being too busy to take the time to learn it. Most women that I have met through LinkedIn tell me they were dragged into it because their boss made them do it, or it was part of their job description. Now, I realize this could be a huge generalization, but that is the response I get from most of the women I have personally chatted with about LinkedIn. They're all on Facebook, but the women I'm associated with don't use LinkedIn very much. When I give my elevator speech at networking meetings, I always ask about LinkedIn. I ask for a show of hands from those who are on LinkedIn and most of the hands in the room are raised. Then I ask how many have their profile at 100%: maybe 20-30% of the hands go up. Then I ask how many have been on their LinkedIn to post something in the last week: about half of the hands go up. Then I ask how many have been on LinkedIn in the last 24 hours: and perhaps one or two hands will go up. I have noticed that most of the women don't raise their hands after I start asking about the 100% completeness and posting weekly or daily. So, if you are one of the exceptions to the rule, "according to findings by Christine Till," you are in the top 2% of women who are active on LinkedIn.

It has been my honour to work with people who are teachable and pleased when they finally see how they can use LinkedIn to benefit themselves and their businesses. I love watching their expressions when they realize for the first time, "I found someone who wants my product."

As a result of doing some one-on-one coaching, I have received requests to teach workshops about using LinkedIn. There were several people who were enthusiastic to help me set up and complete my first workshop in Vancouver, British Columbia. Twelve people attended my first workshop. Three were women and the rest were men. At the break, two attendees Allan Knight and Vince Millardo (both business coaches) said they were having challenges keeping up and from their standpoint could see there wasn't going to be enough time to get through the program in one evening. They offered me their boardroom to conduct a full day workshop. Then, people could bring their laptops and have a system in place when they left at the end of the day.

We completed that first workshop and shortly after the three of us got together to outline a new full day workshop. We also discussed an agenda and while we were discussing this new workshop the idea evolved to have three different workshops. Each three hour module would cover only a small area of the LinkedIn training; thus, one session evolved into three.
Module One: LinkedIn Profile 101

This workshop covers everything to do with setting up a professional, larger than life profile. We learn how to write a gripping summary and how to list our websites so search engines can find us on LinkedIn. We also learn tricks about how to complete our profiles; therefore, search engines can find us if people don't know our name or our company name.

Module Two: LinkedIn Intermediate 202

In this workshop we learn how to connect without being connected and how to get recommendations without asking for them. A written recommendation carries far more weight than simply giving someone an endorsement. I have so many people who have endorsed me! I don't know half of them. So, I wonder, what weight does an endorsement carry? We also start learning how to get set up to "mine" LinkedIn for leads. We learn the secrets of "the groups".

Module Three: LinkedIn Advanced 303

Here we take our LinkedIn marketing to a whole new level with templates we can use for our marketing and surveys to help create connections and build relationships. Now we bring together everything from 101 and 202 to set up our own LinkedIn marketing plan. We also learn how to connect all our social media through an auto-responder to help save time and manage our on-line marketing.

Once I had the three workshops outlined it became apparent that there also needed to be a workbook. As I spoke with my publisher, Julie Salisbury, the vision of publishing my workbook along with my book became apparent. It was one thing to publish this book and speak about what I did, but people really need to have the step-by-step process in a written form that they can use right there in my workshops. Then, they have a tangible outline to take home and refer to on a regular basis.

I first met Allan Knight at a High Output Business Networking meeting. It so happened that I had the opportunity to give my elevator speech before he did. In fact, I think he purposely positioned himself so he would be the last speaker of the morning. ("The gospel according to Christine.") When he stood up to speak, he mentioned two of us and proceeded to give us compliments about how we spoke up and addressed everyone in the room using eye contact. His comments made my day! Since then Allan has been a guest on The Marketing Mentress show. We have built a great business relationship and I value his thoughts and ideas regarding business. Allan was also instrumental in helping me develop my three LinkedIn workshops. I have asked Allan Knight to write a contribution here. Thank you, Allan.

Allan Knight

Thank you Christine Till for considering me as one of your contributors for this great book that will help so many people. You have asked me to write about the challenges of middle agers today in this ever-changing fast paced world, so here it goes.

The first thing I would like to say when it comes to a matter of age, is most of us get way too hung up on the number. At the end of the day, the challenges we face as we get older have less to do with the number or the fact that time is passing us by, but much more to do with our mindset and the process. The challenge of getting older is more about how we manage stress and change in our lives. It's about how we deal with our reaction to the idea of getting older and in the way we face new challenges that come our way.

Many of us were brought up believing that success and happiness would come easily by getting a good education and a job. However valuable these may be, true success is less about what we can control externally and more about how we respond to what we can't control. A former friend of mine was a multi-millionaire who among other things owned a 23-room mansion. He certainly had control over his financial success and wealth, but when it came to attracting a quality relationship he never succeeded. An important part of that was because he couldn't control and master his inner thoughts and feelings about himself. He was actually quite insecure around the women he found attractive. He often sabotaged the relationships by talking too much and turning them off with his perceived self-centredness.

Being happy when things are going well is easy, but it's also about how we act when faced with difficult obstacles and challenges. I like to call these the scud missiles of life. For example, when my twin soul sister Suzie was diagnosed with terminal cancer over five years ago I considered that to be the biggest challenge I had ever faced in my life. In witnessing someone I adored battle pain and death I had a choice to fall to my negative thoughts and emotions or pick myself up by the bootstraps and maintain a great attitude and joyful spirit throughout the process for both our sakes, mostly for Suzie's. As a result, instead of her having to see me down in the dumps, we were actually able to have some of the most wonderful times together.

The scud missiles can be minor, medium or major in nature. Suzie's death was a major one for me. If I can turn lemon into lemonade from that situation, I would suggest that any mid life challenges we may face should be much easier to manage and master. It's all relative. Last year I was invited to a major motivational event including ten highly successful speakers. By far the best speaker on stage was a gentleman named Sean Stephenson. (I highly recommend looking him up on You Tube.) Sean is literally one foot tall and was given 72 hours to live at his time of birth. He is now in his 30's, he's just got married and was the most dynamic and funniest speaker I've ever heard. If Sean, with his extreme circumstances, can rise to the occasion with a winning mindset, how difficult can it be for most of us to go through the much smaller challenges of mid life change?

The reality is that we are living in a very fast changing world. Many of us are either losing our jobs or choosing to be in our own businesses. In order to survive and flourish we need to do the same thing Sean Stephenson did: stop feeling sorry for ourselves and make a commitment to do whatever it takes to be happy and successful. I will leave you with four key pillars that have served me well.

1. VISION - everything begins by getting clear on what it is we really want to do. We can do this by brainstorming by ourselves or with others. Once we're clear, we can decide whether we can begin right away or need to work towards it on a long-term basis. A clear vision is a great foundation and motivator for achieving success.

2. MOTIVATION - having a positive mindset and practicing self-mastery is critical to securing our long-term success. If we're to succeed at a high level, we will have to become ever more effective in building great relationships with others. To do this I feel we have to first master the relationship we have with ourselves. Christine Till doesn't just impact people with her ideas and wisdom, it's her enthusiasm, passion, and personality that really impacts people. That is electromagnetic energy that radiates from within her and that is why it's so important to give attention to our self-development.

3. ACTION - with a clear vision and a great attitude and mindset, we are ready for an action plan and accountability system that will help us stay on track. Ideas and vision are great, but unless there is consistent, focused, and prioritized action, very little will be achieved. Self-confidence is built internally through inner fitness, but also through achievement in the outer world.

4. COMMUNICATION - the first three points are the groundwork and cornerstones for effective communication with others. I have found that approximately 20% of communication has to do with content and technique; however, about 80% has to do

with the passion and energy that oozes out of you. With the mindset and self mastery achieved in number two, you can listen better, have more compassion, inspire more and in general be more effective in all your relationships because you have such a great relationship with yourself.

If you focus on all four pillars on a consistent basis you will achieve what you set out to do. I hope these few words have helped you along on your journey toward true happiness and success.

Allan Knight M.Ed.
www.knighttalk.com
www.allanknight.com

Now, I would like to tell you a story my father told my siblings and I about: The Progressive Farmer.

At the end of the harvest the progressive farmer always kept his machinery in a shed, serviced, and in good repair. In addition his buildings, fences, and feedlots were painted and in good repair. His barns were cleaned regularly and the animals were fed and cared for at a regular time every day. He could count on his breakfast being served promptly at seven o'clock in the morning, lunch served promptly at noon, and dinner served promptly at six o'clock. This progressive farmer could plan his daily chores on a regular schedule, because everyone who worked on his farm was prompt.

Now, the non-progressive farmer was another story. In the spring, when it was time to get ready to plant the crops for the new season, his tractor was sitting in the middle of his hay field from where it had broken down in the fall. As a result, he had to pull the tractor into his shop to get it serviced and repaired. It had rusted from sitting outside all winter and had to be taken to the repair shop in town where he ended up paying a lot of money. His fences were never painted; let alone his barn or any out buildings. The gates were barely hanging on their hinges in the corrals and the animals were skinny because they weren't fed properly. His meals were never ready on time; nothing was planned or scheduled.

Can you see what the difference was, other than the obvious?

The progressive farmer was always trusted to do what he said he would do. The non-progressive farmer was never asked to be on any community committees, because he wasn't reliable. He always had an excuse for being late, missing meetings or events. Consequently, the progressive farmer had a better credit rating as well. Do you know why the progressive farmer had better credit? You guessed it: His bills were paid on time. This may seem like a fairytale to you, but you know who the progressive farmer was? My father!

I share this analogy because it can be applied to all businesses and farming is a business. How are you running your business? Are you like the progressive farmer? How well are you selling yourself? Are you excited about your business when you meet with people and speak about your business at meetings? You are your business. My advice is always to remember that.

The first time I heard the term "selling yourself" was from a speaker at a networking event: I thought it was referring to a lady of the night. No kidding. Anyway, as the lecture continued I asked myself, do I like sales? Am I in sales? Do I like meeting people? How do people react to me? I came to the conclusion that, like it or not, I was in the business of selling myself every waking minute of every day of my life. Therefore, it's up to me to learn how to sell my services and myself. The minute I signed my name on that dotted line to be in business for myself, I became my company's own best salesman.

Have you ever watched a baby? They are perfect salesmen. They know their target audience: mom and dad. They know how to manipulate their target audience within a few short weeks of taking their first breath of life. Babies are experts at getting what they want. There is one flaw in their sales process though, their sale is only "me" centred. I don't believe I'm the only one to have made this blunder in my business. In the past I reached out to my connections thinking solely about me because I really needed to get a sale. I discovered people pick up on that in a big hurry. They were repulsed by my words and actions. Everything I did told them I'm desperate and that I wasn't thinking about what they need. Through my life journey in the business world I have come to realize that it's all about them. It's not about me. Now that I have transferred my traditional sales and marketing to on-line, I have had to realize that it is still all about them.

Mr. Robin J. Elliott taught me a very important lesson. I met Robin in May of 2008. We were meant to meet. Here is what happened. My husband and I were in a local book store looking through the self-help section (As we did on many an occasion, I guess we have had a lot of self-learning to accomplish in our lives). Well, he was on one side of the bookshelf and I was on the other when he exclaimed, "Look what I found!"

I quickly went around to see what it was. He showed me a ticket to attend a meeting in Vancouver about joint ventures. The ticket was free. We wondered if it was a coupon included with the book, but when we checked the rest of the books they didn't have any tickets in them. We decided to check the entire bookshelf, but again we didn't find any more tickets. He looked at me and I looked back at him and we thought about our discovery. Finally I said, "It must be a sign." We both agreed. The ticket was to an event, taking place that very same week. We decided to attend. After all, what did we have to lose?

We walked into the venue, met a lot of enthusiastic people and were invited to sit down to watch the presentation. Robin J. Elliott then proceeded to open our eyes to the future of business. Since then, Robin and his wife Rika have become our dear friends and mentors. I am honoured to have Robin write a special contribution for my book. Robin has written and published 13 books. To this day, I use his book "Joint Ventures for Life" in my business.

I believe the day of the job is gone. From what I've seen people are coming together in groups and setting up memorandums of understanding where they refer each other and pay commissions to each other based on their agreement. I recommend reading Robin J Elliott's book. Robin contributed to my book to assist with other people in similar circumstances to mine. This is his contribution.

Thank you, Robin.

Fifties and Frightened? Sixties and Scared?

Thousands of years ago, people were scared of witches, demons and falling off the end of the Earth until they gained knowledge and understanding. Not knowing what to do, where to turn, or how to handle something is scary. Fear is, indeed, false expectations appearing real – unless you don't have a solution. And unfortunately most solutions are not what they seem to be; in fact many are thinly disguised scams designed to steal what little time and money you do have in order to line the pockets of bad people. Or you need loads of time and money or a massive database, and even then, you could fail dismally.

We've all been ripped off, disappointed, and deceived. The wrong approach is to become so cynical and skeptical that we discount even the good suggestions. Don't let your pessimism and fear rob you of solid advice that can change your life. Take off the judge's robes, open your mind, and objectively evaluate what I have to say. Especially since the proven solution I offer entails no cost or risk, and even more importantly, there aren't any limits of how much you can earn or how fast you can earn it. Remember, no cost or risk: that means this can't be network marketing or investing. And it's definitely not real estate or selling your time, because those contain both risk and limitations. Hear me out.

I'm an unusual kind of entrepreneur: I hate risk. That's why I have stayed in business for 25 years and why I could start all over in a new country as a new immigrant at the age of 45. I'm all about starting over. I lived in eighteen places by the time I was seventeen. I lost everything in a divorce. I got into my own business at 34 and immigrated to Canada at 45. I am now fifty-nine and my system works. I've retired twice using it and I have helped others make millions of dollars. Those facts should encourage you. Plus, your background, education, and age are not a limitation. You can be 65, fresh out of prison, in debt, covered in tattoos, and you can still use this system to create financial freedom.

You probably feel you have limited time, limited money, less energy, and perhaps even some health problems. The cliché "Time is running out" may be going around in your head. Well, it is running out if you think in conventional money-making terms, but this is a different approach. Let's look at what you have going for you: all your strengths, assets, relationships, resources, experience, the credibility and wisdom of age, and all your skills and abilities. Focus on your strengths and what you have and want, instead of your weaknesses, what you can't do, what you don't have, and what you don't want. Let's look at what you can do, and what is possible. Y-A-H-O-O means You Always Have Other Options. It's not too late.

What do we want? Remember this: You don't need millions of dollars in the bank. You simply need more income every month than you need to live on. And you'll be surprised at how simple the system is. The wealthiest people on earth have multiple income streams from diverse sources (not all their eggs in one basket). They don't sell their time, and they use leverage. Instead of buying, you can borrow what someone else already has. Instead of creating, you can piggyback on what is already created. If you could have just a little piece of the profit of each of ten different businesses, you could earn some serious money.

If you introduce someone to a product or a service, the person or business selling that product or service should pay you a commission or compensate you in some way. That's simple reciprocity. I scratch your back, you scratch mine. Everyone has needs, wants, goals, and problems. They need solutions and those solutions come in the form of products or services sold by people and businesses. You've probably referred thousands of people to useful products and services in the past, and you have probably, in most cases, not even earned a thank you in return. Why not get paid?

If you were to approach a savvy business and ask them to pay you a commission for people you refer (who end up buying their product or service) you're offering them the opportunity to make more money and to pay you for results: not promises. They only pay you for sales made. They would rather earn 90% of a sale than 100% of nothing, right? If they don't want to pay or compensate you in an acceptable way, move on. There are literally millions of businesses to talk with and you can do this on the phone, on the Internet, or in person.

Next, ask them to share some of their marketing material or systems with you: brochures, gift certificates, flyers, webinars, free consultations, and so forth. They will come up with some really ingenious way for you to introduce their products and services, including affiliate programs. I specialize in brick and mortar businesses, not Internet sales, since there are some dishonest people on the Internet and it's hard to check. Now you have been equipped with some useful tools at no cost to you. Remember: no cost, no risk. You can use these tools when introducing and recommending products and services to people.

Let me share some real life, practical examples of how

I teach my business owner clients to use Joint Venture Leverage to make more money. Consider how these simple, yet powerful ideas can be adapted to fit your life and circumstances. I think it's easier to understand this concept by hearing how others have used them and continue to do so.

One thing that works really well is gift certificates. So many of my clients provide people with these vouchers; for example, a signage business prints gift certificates entitling the holder or recipient with a free, 3' by 2' canvas print of a photograph. No obligation, no purchase necessary. People (like you) can hand these gift certificates to business owners who (when they meet and interact with the signage company to get their beautiful canvas prints) often end up buying signs and the person giving away the gift certificates then receives 10% commissions on all the purchases which can be anywhere from a few hundred dollars to thousands of dollars. And each time they buy more signs, the person who gave them the gift certificate gets paid – that means ongoing, passive income. No cost or risk to the person giving away the gift certificates.

Another one of my clients offers gift certificates entitling the holder to a half hour of free electrolysis hair removal, valued at $75. Most people who take them up on this free sample service become clients and the person issuing the gift certificate will then receive a one-time payment of $50. This same client will pay you a six thousand dollar commission if you refer someone to her who buys a hair removal franchise or invests in one. She also speaks about women in business. If you were to arrange for her to speak at a Chamber of Commerce, Rotary Club or any other event, she just might end up selling more than one franchise: And you would get $6,000 for every one sold.

You could also sell these gift certificates to restaurants or other businesses for a dollar each. Then, the business giving away gift certificates to their customers can add massive value while differentiating themselves from their competition. Imagine if you worked hard at this, and got good at it, you could end up with ten restaurants each buying 1,000 gift certificates per month. You could sell gift certificates for free haircuts, manicures, self defense classes, gym memberships: you get the picture and the gift certificates would drive people into those businesses. Even if you weren't receiving commission for selling the gift certificates, they could provide you with a lucrative, ongoing income.

You can also triangulate deals. For example, business "A" sends out gift certificates or introductions to business "B" to their clients. Business "B" pays you a commission on all the sales made, which you then share with Business "A." Keep it simple. Peter asks you if you know of a good mechanic. Before introducing him to John, your own trusted mechanic, you ask John if he would be prepared to pay you a commission on any business you bring him. If John agrees, you refer Peter to him. Or John might agree to service your car as a thank you gesture for the business you send him.

You can use contingency advertising as well – have an advertiser place an advert for your Joint Venture Partner's business (someone who you promote in return for commissions on sales made). The people responding to the advert are received by the advertiser and then sent to you, and you, in turn, send them to your JV partner. Then, you share any commissions earned with the advertiser.

I offer a free coaching consultation to business owners and the person making the introduction receives a 10% commission every month. One of my clients uses three services that I referred him to and I get paid commissions on all of them. This is "Back End" income for me – all 100% profit. Uncovered leads can be a gold mine for you, too. You arrange for one business to send you all the leads they didn't convert – people who showed an interest in their product or service but didn't buy for some reason – and you send those leads to another business selling the same or a similar product or service. You get paid on all the sales and you share that commission with the person who sent you the leads in the first place. We even do this between people selling franchises: serious commissions there.

You can also become an agent. My friend is a musician with a neck problem that has prevented him from playing the piano as much as he would like to; therefore, the injury limited the income he could earn while playing. So, he printed business cards and called himself a "Musician's Agent". He visited many bars, restaurants, wedding planners, hotels, and other places that regularly hired musicians. He said, "Call me for whatever musicians you need. I will interview them, make sure they can do the job, and make sure they are replaced in time if they don't show up. There isn't any charge to you for my service because the musicians pay me a portion of what they earn. You don't pay the musicians, you pay me. Then, I deduct my fee and pay the remainder to the musicians."

He then approached good musicians with his proposal and he earned 15% on when he booked them a gig. His income soared. You can be an agent for dog walkers, baby sitters, public speakers (a speakers bureau) you name it. Try to specialize in an industry you know and understand well. Other people do the work: at no cost or risk to you.

I have 47 systems that I use when working with my clients. I tailor make the implementation, but you can see that only a few of them can provide you with financial freedom. You act as a middleman. You connect supply and demand and take a piece of the action. You only get paid for results, but you leverage other people's time, money, resources, businesses, and distribution. A Joint Venture Broker is essentially a paid connector. You get paid for helping others get what they want. There isn't any selling or pressure. You're connecting people anyway: you might as well get paid for it.

You can see the only limit here is your understanding and implementation of this amazing system. The more you learn and do, the more you earn and enjoy. There is no limit, no cost, no risk, and no excuse. If you can't get out of your home, use the phone or the Internet. Don't find an excuse – find a way. You can do this. Use the connections, experience, and other resources you have to make this happen. Believe you can do it. Don't risk your time and money: create multiple Joint Ventures. Don't put all your eggs into one basket. Live frugally and have fun. My favourite slogan is from Paul J. Meyer, who wrote, "Whatever you vividly imagine, ardently desire, sincerely believe, and enthusiastically act upon must inevitably, come to pass."

Remember, knowledge without implementation is useless. We reap what we sow, and massive sowing results in massive reaping. As with anything, it gets easier and you earn more with practice. Make mistakes, enjoy it – you have nothing to lose and everything to gain. Make a game of it. Think big and believe you can do it. With action comes confidence.

I know you probably have many questions. You can grab a free membership and lots of information from my website: www.DollarMakers.com and learn more at www.LeverageAdvantage.com or email me at robin@ dollarmakers.com

Robin J Elliott
www.LeverageAdvantage.com

Chapter Six

Making It Pay

Now, my next learning curve was how could I run my own seminars and learn to make money from them?

Did you know we forget 75% of what we learn in a seminar within the first 24 hours? It's a shame isn't it? From my experience, I try to take scrupulous notes and refer to them after the seminar, but do you know what usually happens? I take those notes and put them in a special file (for later reference) and return to my daily routine while assuming, "I'll refer to them later." I'll leave the file on the top of my desk to remind me; and then an emergency arises; and another file gets placed on top; until finally the seminar notes are buried and I have forgotten all about them. (How Much of Your Presentation will They Remember? By Malcolm Edwards "Researchers once ran a test to measure how much of a presenter's message sticks in the minds of their audience. They found that immediately after a 10-minute presentation, listeners only remembered 50% of what was said. By the next day that had dropped to 25%, and a week later it was 10%.")

One day I decided to tidy my desk to find a particular seminar file. I wanted to open it and review my notes. What did I see? A scribbled mess and I can't remember for the life of me what those notes mean - and here I thought I was carefully taking notes.

It's for this reason that I decided to conduct interactive seminars. I wanted people to bring their laptops, iPads, and implement what I was teaching them on the spot. I wanted people to leave my workshops with a system in place and be ready to work immediately. However, conducting interactive workshops meant that I had to have reliable Internet connections in all my venues. Going live on the Internet has made it a challenge to find locations that have the capacity of supporting 12 to 15 laptops at one time.

Another challenge was to find an affordable location so I could offer my workshop at a reasonable cost to the attendees. I know how it feels to want to attend a workshop, but unable to afford the registration fees. So, I made a concerted effort to keep my prices reasonable while searching out suitable locations. This challenge offered another profound learning experience for me: covering expenses.

By the end of 2011 our finances were dire. We had all our credit cards maxed out and had used up all our savings. My Employment Insurance (EI) had expired in the middle of July 2011. We were living on my husband's income alone. Try as I might, I was unable to monetize the podcasts.

One day I was emailing my brother about my predicament and he suggested I apply for early retirement through my Canada Pension Plan (CPP). I was shocked that anyone would even suggest such a preposterous idea. After all, I wasn't old. Only old people retired: that was the belief I had going through my mind.

I felt my brother thought I was old and at first I felt quite insulted at his suggestion. He explained that his sister-in-law, who was only a year older than me, had found herself in the same position. She applied for early retirement and was sitting pretty. I think she had another pension plan in addition to the Canada Pension Plan; however, I checked it out to see if anything would be available to me. I discovered that CPP would pay me approximately $545 when I reached 65 years of age. If I claimed it now, I would have to take approximately a $200 discount as it would be classified as an early retirement. After thinking through my options, I decided to take an early retirement and at least I would have a little bit of money to cover a few of our costs. The decision was made and I sent in my paperwork.

It's a shame to live a life, work hard, and end up with so little reward for all one's hard work. After everything was processed I made approximately $345 a month from CPP. As I think about it now, it's really depressing. Yet, through all of this I had a feeling that everything would work out. I don't have any idea why I have always felt things would financially work out for us. Even in our darkest hours of desperation, I kept hoping that somehow our ship would come in.

There were times when I would sink pretty deep into feelings of regret. I would ponder about how I could have saved more or how I could have had a better financial plan, but do you know what? I'm not a shopper; I seldom go shopping for anything new. The last time I went and bought a new outfit to wear was September 2008: and I'm still wearing it today. I never wear anything out. Thank goodness I haven't gained a lot of weight. I spent money on bills, groceries, household supplies, the car, and the other monthly expenses we incur.

In the summer of 2011 I was approached by two different people about a new platform called Talk Fusion; webinars. This platform had a masterful way of combining the latest technology with email and newsletters and multiple other marketing platforms. Well, the first exposure I had wasn't impressive, so I disregarded it and put it out of my mind. Then, in February of 2012, I received a video email on Talk Fusion from Allan Knight.

Well, this time it was a different story. This video email impressed me with how professionally it was done. I sent Allan an email immediately and stated that this was the most professional video email I had ever seen using Talk Fusion and I asked him to teach me more about it. I thought if Allan was using this platform, then there must be more to this than I thought. Little did I realize that there had been many improvements made on the Talk Fusion platform since I had first been introduced to it six months beforehand.

We arranged to meet downtown Vancouver and Allan was

going to show me how it worked. He brought his laptop and I recorded my own video. Then he played it back for me to see. Oh my gosh, I was blown away. There I was on television.

Immediately, I saw the potential of this platform. I could see how business owners could use this to help promote their businesses. I had to have it. And to top it all off, I could make a little money on the side too. Bonus.

Allan invited me to watch a webinar on Talk Fusion to learn more about their products and how the money flowed. I fell in love with it and wanted to sign up immediately. So, Allan helped me get signed up.

Now, with Talk Fusion to use for my webinars, I had a new vision for The Marketing Mentress. The webinars I conducted were for people on LinkedIn to receive a few quick tips to make their profile more professional. I was new to this platform and wanted to learn how to maximize it, so I conducted my LinkedIn webinars for free. However, when I conducted them for free they were poorly attended. There is significance in charging a fee for your webinars and workshops, because people will attach value to them.

As I mentioned earlier, by the fall of 2011 I discovered I could trade my podcasting skills for other services such as coaching. Since then, I have been working with two different types of life coaches with whom I've traded podcasting and LinkedIn training. I have become very good at interviewing people and I'm still not perfect, but that will be an ongoing project. The coaches have taught me something significant about life, business, and myself. I now have many dear friends as a result of interviewing them and I'm honoured to have had the opportunity of working with all these wonderful people.

Here are some of the people I have interviewed who have taught me many lessons. I asked them to share their knowledge here.

My sister, Diane Stringam Tolley is an author, speaker, writer, and expert blogger. Diane is considered the "writer" in the family, along with my mother and a brother. However, Diane has had the most articles published in print media and she has published the most books, so we all refer to her as the "family writer". All three have published at least one book; Diane is now on her fifth book. She is my great example when it comes to writing and my inspiration to continue writing.

I have asked Diane Stringam Tolley to share her story.

Thank you, Diane.

My Story
By Diane Stringam Tolley

"We really love your work and we will miss you," she said, "but there is no way we can keep you on." And with those words, my long time career as a bookstore manager ended.

Fifty-two years old and unemployed. Never mind, that it really didn't have anything to do with my abilities or my intelligence. No, it had to do with my knees. Let me explain.

The bookstore was small, taking up two floors, with everything "office" on the second floor. I made fifteen to twenty trips up and down in the course of a day: definitely an action that called for healthy knees. The store owner was right. Nothing short of moving or a complete renovation on their part; or major surgery on mine, could be done. For the first time in my life I hated those joints that had carried me (through sports, marathons, dance instructing, and six children) for fifty-two years. They had finally let me down. Stupid knees. I went through a short time of severe pouting and feeling sorry for myself, then I pulled up my support hose and got to work.

First I made a rather drastic foray into the world of bookkeeping and accounting, because I love numbers.

Well, at least I did love numbers. Let's just say that at the end of seven months, numbers and I bade a not-so-fond farewell and leave it at that.

Back to the diving board. I would have said drawing board, but this was more accurate. I decided to make a list of those abilities that were still left to me. I had work experience from the jobs that had put me through college nearly forty years before: Herdsman 4.0, Patient Care 3, and Burger Flipping 101. I hadn't done any of them in a while, but the jobs looked very similar to what *my* duties had been. Oops! Knees, again. I almost forgot.

I also still had my brain, my journalism certificate, and my Typing 10 abilities. Hmmm, I could still type, and I could still think: two important, and potentially complimentary abilities. That was it, I would write. Whew! That was settled. But write what? I should mention here I have always written stories, articles, books, more stories, and more books. I had received kudos for such practices, but seldom had I received actual monetary gain.

For every advantage, there's a disadvantage. Soooo . . . where could I sell myself, in a totally non-prostitute sense?

Some years ago when I landed the job in the bookstore that I loved so much, there was an amazing device that whisks us around the world in a nano-second. It's a tool that is capable of collecting, holding, and displaying every single writing job being offered in the entire world. You know what I'm talking about: the Internet.

That reigning king among office implements; that must have tool for the modern "looking-for-work-er" and with which I didn't have any experience. Fortunately, I had a willing and able son-in-law who was eager to show me the ropes. Would I say learning about the Internet was surprisingly easy? No. Would I say with the proper motivation it can be done, even after the age of fifty? Yes, definitely it can be done. In a surprisingly short time, I was surfing.

There are literally thousands of writing jobs available on the Internet; for example, did you know that companies hire people to write blogs for them? And there are other companies who want people to become armchair travelers? It's true, with emphasis on the armchair. Companies want people to research their sites and write their impressions based on what they can find on the Internet and what is listed in the actual company blurb. It sounded delicious. I applied for one of those jobs.

Within half an hour I had received a bona fide job offer, with pay and perks - really. Her actual words were, "I don't think I've ever read an application letter quite like that one. You've got the job!"

Now I've finally wound my long-winded way to the point of this entire article.

When applying for a writing job - be creative. Be clever. Be surprising. Be outrageous. But do it in your first line and be brief.

This story can also relate to my friend Penny. She was a mature, returning student, and wanted to get her business teacher's attention. Her class assignment was to draft a job application for a fictitious job. She applied to be his girlfriend. Well, her assignment got his attention: she got the job.

As they taught us in Journalism all those years ago: Your first line should never exceed thirteen words. Therefore, you have thirteen words to get your reader's attention. The line that netted me the job went like this: "Touching sunshine? Hearing music? Tasting and feeling magic? Smelling perfection? You have arrived!" See, thirteen words. It can be done and you can do it.

Here are some of the sites I visited in my search:
www.simplyhired.ca/a/jobs/list/q-writing
www.online-writing-jobs.com

www.freelancewritinggigs.com
www.wowjobs.ca/BrowseResults.aspx?q=Writer
vancouverwritingjobs.com
ca.indeed.com/Technical-Writer-jobs-in-Calgary-AB
weblogs.about.com/od/professionalblogging
BloggingJobs
jobs.problogger.net
www.freelancer.ca/jobs/Travel-Writing
www.women-on-the-road.com

There are literally hundreds, even thousands of these sites. Just type "Writer Jobs" or "Blogging Jobs" or "Travel Writer Jobs" into the search bar and press enter. The magical mystery of the Internet (that I will never hope to understand) comes to life and hunts for exactly what you need.

Remember: Give them something they haven't heard before and you'll be in.

Diane Stringam Tolley
Author
Carving Angels 2011
Kris Kringle's Magic 2012
www.dianestringamtolley.com
www.dlt-lifeontheranch.blogspot.com
dtolley@shaw.ca

Brigitte Dunbar came into my life through the promotional products industry. She ordered some embroidered shirts through me for her business. Then, when I was working in the senior care industry we met again. In a way, she was my competition. She is the owner of a business called "Driving Miss Daisy." It is a business that has cute little cars with chauffeurs who pick up seniors and take them to their appointments, go shopping, or take care of any other needs they may have. We have become good friends over the years and I asked her to share her story with us.

Brigitte Dunbar, owner of a Driving Miss Daisy franchise, has openly shared her story with us.

Thank you, Brigitte!

Brigitte Dunbar's Story

I felt a real need to be able to connect with people. I didn't want to spend my time in front of a computer or at a desk. For me, I discovered working with seniors and having daily interactions with people has made a difference in my life.

Since high school, I had been employed as a legal secretary for over 25 years. Although I was content with my personal life, my working life was getting too stressful and too unmanageable. I was working at a busy law firm for a workaholic boss, a mother to three, and losing two hours a day on public transit. I wasn't happy and my need to connect with others wasn't being met. As my children got older I realized I could do something else and serve humanity.

The evolution of my career changes was simple. It all started with a co-worker whose father was ill and subsequently passed away. She was taking her parents to medical appointments and assisting with their needs while still trying to work and cooperate with her boss. At the same time, my father-in-law had been diagnosed with inoperable cancer and ultimately went to the hospice to live out his days. My colleague and I had heard about bad experiences with taxi drivers and we thought "if a nice lady was able to pick up our parents and take them where they needed to go" that would be a wonderful option for them.

As my career dissatisfaction grew, I steadily poured through the help wanted ads hoping for something that would change my working life. One day, in the business section of the Vancouver Sun, there was an article about Bev Halisky, who had opened "Driving Miss

Daisy" in Alberta and was successful. She was now bringing the idea to British Columbia and was looking for franchise owners. I immediately contacted her and arranged a meeting.

Our first meeting went well. After much thought and discussion with my husband, we decided to take a leap of faith and purchase this new-to-BC franchise business. The idea is simple, assist seniors in your area to get where they need to go in the Lower Mainland. They trust us to get them from their living room to the doctor's office or anywhere else they need to go. Of course, experience has shown that there are innumerable needs in the life of a senior, so I have done much more than get them to their medical appointments.

I am so much happier in my life. My work experience in the legal liability field, with all of the stories of accidents that could have been prevented, has taught me so much about people and their needs. The transition into my new career felt natural. The work has been hard at times and certainly no gratitude at other times, but I knew I was doing the right thing when one of my first clients was a veteran who was needing to visit his wife in a full term care facility. During World War Two his regiment had participated in the liberation of the Netherlands. My parents are grateful Dutch immigrants who will never forget the Canadian soldiers who saved them. I felt then and still do and this is my own way of honouring those seniors for their sacrifice all those years ago. Life has a strange way of turning around sometimes.

It has now been over four years since my husband and I invested in the franchise. I have learned a lot. I have encountered a steep drop in my salary, but personally and professionally I'm satisfied. It has been gratifying to know I participate in supporting seniors to live their lives the way they wish.

I feel my contribution towards seniors and assisting

them to continue to live the lives they choose has made all the difference in my working life. I own my business; thus, I get the satisfaction of choosing which direction I wish to go; how long I wish to continue something; and which customers to assist. I set my own hours and provide all types of services to those who need assistance.

When I reflect back I was so unhappy and stressed out at work. It was so bad that as I watched a car driving towards me one day I thought, "If I had a car accident, I would have an excuse not to go to work." That was a huge wake up call for me. If work was bringing me down so much that a car accident was my alternative, a change was needed.

I didn't get fired from my job. I was unhappy and looking for a change. The satisfaction of having made a change on my own is great; however, everyone's frame of mind is important and each person chooses what they like to do to provide for themselves and their families.

Naturally, no job is perfect. We all have days when we wish to simply relax on a beach and have servants do everything for us, but that is just for a while and then it's back to work. When a person is happy with their career, happiness and satisfaction can spill over to other areas of life: it certainly has in mine.

Negative attitudes and thoughts can really take over when things aren't going well. Positive attitudes and thoughts can spread as well, but in a healthy way where we can help others and make good changes in their lives.

I must also take this opportunity to stress that from my experience, mature workers are reliable, conscientious, hard-working, and have common sense. Even before I quit working for the law firm, I noted that the young lawyers and staff members didn't work the extra hours to get things done. We mature workers have a duty that

gets jobs done. (The gospel according to Brigitte)
I am definitely a better, happier, and a more rounded person with the changes I have made in my life.
Brigitte Dunbar
www.drivingmissdaisy.net

What do you have in your toolbox that you could trade for services?

I have discovered that I have a few, but my best tool is LinkedIn. Since I was fired, LinkedIn has always been my specialty. My son taught me the basics and since then I have learned much more.

You can join groups on LinkedIn. Actually, I feel the secret to LinkedIn is in the groups and not many people know this. I have joined a lot of groups. LinkedIn only allows you to join fifty groups, I'm already at my limit. When you reach your limit of fifty groups, you can always unjoin some groups so you can join some new ones. However, when it comes to sub-groups, you can join as many as you want. There aren't any limits on joining sub-groups. The key is to join the groups that have ten thousand members or more. Remember, you want to "mine" LinkedIn through the groups. It is in the groups where you will find your potential target audience. I learned that lesson the hard way. I was joining groups that were fun and I was getting involved in their discussions. However, I soon found that I could not keep up with 50 groups. I now only have about three groups that I interact with on a regular basis. The rest I just use for "mining".

One of these groups was a LinkedIn Open Networker (LION) group. I became attached and involved in their discussions because that group had more depth than just people wanting to connect with people. If you are a LION that means that you will connect with anyone who asks to connect with you without IDKing anyone (IDK means I Don't Know you). If your account receives 5 IDK's, then it will be suspended. One thing you never want to do on LinkedIn is invite people you don't know to connect with you unless you are in a LION group. In a LION group everyone will accept your connection request without any IDKs. I learned this one the hard way.

While in my favourite LION group, I noticed there were many professional people wanting to connect with other professionals, but many of them had pretty shabby looking profiles. With LinkedIn being a professional platform, one needs to make sure that your profile is at 100% complete and that everything on your profile makes you look larger than life. It's also important that key elements are in place in your profile to help search engines find you there. I have seen many Website gurus and SEO specialists miss this big time.

When I say "a shabby looking profile" I'm referring to the profile missing some key elements; for example, no headshot or using a company logo in place of a headshot. Your company logo is not you.

When there isn't a headshot on the profile, subconsciously it's telling people that the person is hiding something and most people hesitate to connect with these headless profiles. There is another important factor involved here too; we human beings want to be connected with other human beings, not an entity or a logo.

Well, my son got a brainwave of doing lead generation through the use of social media and after discussing it with him, we decided to see what we could come up with. To this day we are using social media for lead generation.

Our process of lead generation is labour intensive and yet very targeted, because we can target specific markets for our clients. We are able to hand over highly qualified leads to our clients and our clients are willing to pay for them. However, our best clients are ones with high-ticket items for sale. Our leads are too expensive for the average solopreneur business because our lead generation is very labour intensive. At times we have hired people from overseas to help with the workload and the lead generation.

As I was attending the networking meetings, I would watch the people sitting around the tables. I noticed that 60-70% of the people attending these meetings had grey hair or were bald. I began to realize that these people had probably found themselves in exactly the same position as I did. They found themselves out of work and struggling to find a way to offer value to society and monetize themselves. I wondered how I could help all those people. I knew they couldn't afford to pay for the lead generation that my son and I were doing.

Suddenly, it dawned on me that I could teach people how to do what we were doing for themselves. I was using LinkedIn to get clients. I could teach people how to use LinkedIn to get clients too! I could start conducting workshops and webinars to teach our secrets to people.

So, how can you make your LinkedIn convert? Once I realized I had been using my own LinkedIn to find people to interview and find clients to do lead generation, I realized I was converting my LinkedIn into sales. If the people I met at the networking meetings couldn't afford my services, then I could teach them to do what I was doing on a smaller scale, for themselves. Now, this is what I teach in my workshops and private coaching sessions. The details of LinkedIn will be covered in my LinkedIn workbook set to be published in the spring of next year, 2013.

You can check out some of our LinkedIn Secrets on YouTube.
LinkedIn Secrets I – Don't Be Bashful; Tell All
www.youtube.com/watch?v=70qJjS9AmUQ
LinkedIn Secrets II – Never Send Connection Invitations
www.youtube.com/watch?v=-EWM-jghoKw
LinkedIn Secrets III – Groups Are the Key to Networking
www.youtube.com/watch?v=_7MO1HV2CpI

My email is now up to 200+ a day. I think it's about time I turned off some group emails. I can't read that many emails in a day and get any work done. I could spend my entire day and late into the evening with just my email. What I do is schedule two times a day to check my email for one hour maximum.

Now, moving on to Facebook. For eight years I hesitated to join Facebook and do you know why? I read their entire Terms of Use Agreement. It says that Facebook reserves the right to use your information and your pictures to how they see fit. Once you upload anything on that platform, it becomes the "property of Facebook," and basically you lose ownership.

I thought that was invasive, rude, and obnoxious to say the least. How could they be so crass? I wanted to protect my information. Here is a caveat: I have discovered that the more you're on the Internet with your face and your name, the less chance you have of being phished or having your identity stolen. Too many people know you and who you are.

Finally, in the spring of 2009, I opened up my first Facebook account … kicking and screaming. I discovered it's a fun platform and much more simplistic than LinkedIn. I like it to keep in touch with my children and the rest of my family. Now, I have two personal profiles and four business pages on Facebook. I have been enjoying watching how many people "Like" my pages and learning how to invite people. I could spend most of my day just fiddling with my Facebook now.

The main reason I'm on Facebook is because all the social media marketing gurus out there say we should have a Facebook page. I use them for different things. One is for my Talent Management; one is for my Practical Podcasting; one is for my BC Marketing Mentress; one is for The Marketing Mentress.

Now, I also manage Facebook and Twitter accounts for other companies. I mentioned earlier that Facebook is like the company barbeque. It's less professional and the average annual income of people over 19 years of age on Facebook is about $25-30K. This is a vast difference from the average annual income of the people on LinkedIn. You need to be able to reach people on many different levels, so with a personal profile on Facebook, as well as a business page (Brand Page) you can reach your friends and their friends. By inviting people to "Like" your Facebook Brand Page, you can connect with people on a more professional level through Facebook. I love Facebook's Brand Pages. The changes Facebook has made to allow people to connect their Brand Pages and readily invite people to events that you are sponsoring is awesome.

Something we need to think seriously about regarding our Facebook Brand Page is how to make it different from our profile page. Our business page needs a more professional, attention-grabbing application. Did you know that 90% of people who "Like" your Facebook Brand Page never come back?

Now, I'd like to share the three second rule of Facebook.

First: Keep it fun and engaging. Nobody wants to come visit you if you are boring. Use lots of pictures.

Second: Ask questions that people will want to respond to. Be controversial.

Third: You need 25 "Likes" to get your analytics started on Facebook. This is where Google will recognize you, and so will Facebook and other platforms. It's like your "seal of credibility".

Fourth: Use coupons and or Facebook ads to target your market and entice your audience.

If you have not captured the attention of prospective customers using these four steps, either you need to rethink your campaign or you are not targeting your market properly.

That's the Facebook gospel according to Christine.

Are you on Facebook yet? Do you have a personal profile and a Brand Page? If you need help setting this up, feel free to connect with me on Facebook and like me at www.facebook.com/themarketingmentress.

What about Twitter? I mentioned earlier that Twitter is like the coffee shop meeting. Many people 45+ don't understand Twitter or how to use it properly. I started to use it because the social media marketing gurus said I should. However, much to my surprise, I discovered that you actually can meet great people on this platform and even create a buzz that attracts business.

With Twitter you need to be interacting with other people up to 15 times a day. Yes, you heard me correctly. I said fifteen times a day. Here is how you break it down: I mentioned earlier that you need to post at least four times a day on all your platforms (LinkedIn, Facebook, Twitter). You can even schedule posts up to eight times a day on all these platforms of social media. These posts must be original material though. You don't just post quotes from Abe Lincoln, for instance. You post what is relevant to your business, but don't sound "salesy". Grab your followers' interest; ask for their help. People love to help.

However, Twitter is instant. People will see your posted tweet come through on their computer/iPad/iPhone/etc., and if it catches their eye they'll respond back. The first great practice is to thank people for following you on Twitter. Oh, by the way a tweet is what you call the comments and posts that you send out on the Twitter platform. I mentioned earlier that these are 140 characters in length, including the URLs you might send in them to get people to your Facebook page for a "Like" or your LinkedIn page to connect, or your Twitter handle to follow you. Remember, if you are asking people to come to your different platforms always think about what they will find when they go to your platforms. Are they going to find something that is engaging?

How is your Twitter doing? Have you thanked someone for following you on twitter today? How many Tweets have you made today?

This is where your blog comes into play. What is a blog? I wondered this myself. I discovered a blog is a short article around 250 to 750 words in length. These articles are engaging and fun to read. They can be about any topic of your choice; however, I caution you to keep your blog business centred. Try not to digress. Keep the attention of your readers focused on your blog through ideas that will capture their attention. There is one main caveat here: never pitch through your blog. You merely create interest and a desire to keep following your blog posts.

There are many free platforms you can use for your blog. My first recommendation in "Blogs according to Christine" would be to use your own website for your blog, similar to the way I use mine. You may not have a podcast show, but you can post your blog on your website in similar fashion. By using your website, you save yourself from having to go to a separate platform and you are visiting your website regularly. So many people set up their website and then seldom revisit it. By revisiting your website regularly, you're alerted to responses on your blog posts and all the other little things that need tweaking from time to time.

Through your blog, you can even be a little transparent. Share with people a blooper you made with your business, a lesson learned on how to treat a customer, or whatever you feel is relevant. If you are a new business, you could write about how you decided to start your business. Remember, people want to know more about you and who you are and why you do what you do. They want to find out what your mission is.

Your blog should be the centre of all your social media: if you use it properly. My centre blog is my website. I post all my blogs on my website. These are the blogs that I write for each person I interview on my show. My blogs are about business and what inspired people to go into the type of business they have and what kinds of marketing work best for them. You can check my blogs out at www.practicalpodcasting.com.

A blog is written around topics that are pertinent to your business. Your blog has a URL that you can attach to your posts; thus, when you send it out on Twitter you can use less than 140 characters. However, your Facebook and LinkedIn platforms will read this URL and expand the post to fit their platforms by displaying the picture and title of your blog post as well.

Pictures and videos are extremely important to consider when writing your blogs. I don't know how much people read any more. We tend to scan the headlines and if something catches our attention, we linger, or watch on.

How often should you post a new blog? The absolute minimum is once a week. The best is three times a week, Monday, Wednesday, Friday or Tuesday, Thursday, Saturday. If you are using Sprout Social for your auto-responder, you can see instantly which days are optimal for you to be posting your blog. At first, you need to experiment with different days. Within a couple weeks, you'll see who is reading your blog, what days they're reading and what the demographics are. If you see your readership drop off at some point, review what you are writing in your blog and try posting on different days of the week.

I keep rotating my blog posts on different days of the week, but I find that I get the most views on Tuesday, Wednesday, and Thursday. The reason I keep posting to different days is because I interview a variety of different businesses and those businesses attract varied demographics, not necessarily the same as mine.

What is your blog about? How often do you post? Send me your URL. I would love to read it and help in any way, if you like. (christine@practicalpodcasting.com)

Chapter Seven

The Second Tsunami

For most of my life I have thought of myself as a plain Jane. I was unpopular in school, called "the witch" in grade three, and never really accepted after that. My mom worked hard to teach me how to groom myself, to be fit, and to watch my calorie intake. I have been on a diet since I was nine years old and it led me to becoming bulimic by the time I was 15 years old. I would eat and then purge. Afterwards I would wash my face, brush my teeth and gargle with mouthwash so no one could suspect me.

My depression was deep. I would start to eat ice cream, chocolate cake, or chocolate chip cookies and I wouldn't stop until the container was empty. After that I would drink a couple glasses of water and stick a toothbrush down my throat to trigger the purge. I had no idea what was wrong with me. In those days, people didn't think children and teenagers need counselling to cope with their emotional challenges. We just went through life sucking it up.

One day I happened to be walking past the bathroom when my mom was inside. I heard similar purging sounds. At first I thought she was sick or something. I never thought she might have the same challenges as me. When she came out I asked her if she was okay. She said she was fine. I queried her about purging. My mom then confessed that she had eaten too much and had to get rid of it. I asked her how long she had been doing this and she said since she was a teenager. I don't think I ever told my mom I was doing the same thing. I still have bulimic symptoms today, but I never purge because tiny blood vessels burst around my eyes and I look like I have two black eyes. That is the only thing that stops me today.

I gained 30 pounds in my first semester of college. My roommates and I were living on macaroni and cheese. When I went home for Christmas people said they didn't recognize me. I cried and cried. That's when I became determined never to eat anything but one dish of ice cream for lunch and dinner and nothing else. That was a bright idea. I broke out in the worst acne and became skinny. The skinny part I loved, but my inner thighs still touched when I stood with my legs together, so I was determined to lose more weight until my thighs didn't touch. Imagine that? Here I was, an emotional mess. I couldn't tell my parents about my feelings for fear of being scolded. Concurrently, I couldn't stop for fear of getting fat. Of course, I never told my doctor either for fear of him scolding me too. You see, down deep inside I knew what I was doing wasn't right, but I was stuck between knowing what was right and wanting to be beautiful and accepted by my peers. I wonder how many people there are in the world today who are experiencing these same feelings and getting stuck. Could it be you?

Earlier I mentioned how the crisis of being fired at fifty brought up ugly demons from my past. Well, it caused me to face these demons and deal with them: forever. I have been blessed with being able to barter my podcasting and LinkedIn coaching services with Monika Becker and Sheryl Stanton: two of the best life coaches in the world in my humble opinion.

I'm now feeling happy in my own body. I would still like to lose 20 pounds, but due to the trauma I have put my body through over the years every time I try to start another diet I get panicky because my body knows the suffering I have put it through. Mentally, I just can't go there again. What I have learned to do is to find a system that works for me. I exercise regularly. I alternate between my twist board and therabands at home. Plus, I go swimming to keep fit and stay slim, but mostly to stay slim. It's the self-preservation discipline I have now.

I worked with a fitness coach who taught me to calculate the number of calories that are optimal for me to lose weight on a daily basis. The driving force behind my fitness ethic is to keep slim. I can't just sit around, because I can't fathom the thought of ever being fat. That said, I still want to shed a few pounds. My fitness coach advises me to exercise and it will come off as long as I stick to my eating regimen.

So, here I was making an impact on society through my social media and not really understanding why I was attracting people to me. I believed I had to be the hardest working woman alive in order to attract followers. Well, humbly speaking, that is correct. I'll bet that some of you have been going through similar things with regard to self-image, haven't you?

When I met Julie Salisbury from Influence Publishing and she invited me to attend her InspireABook Intensive workshop, it was only then I realized I could help other people in the same situation by sharing my story. I had considered writing a book but I didn't know if my story was interesting enough or my writing good enough. Julie inspired me to look back on my own journey and help other people going through the same experience. It is an amazing process! I walked in on the first day of the workshop with my outline all ready. Plus, I had written almost a full chapter. My title was, "Enhancing Your Personal Marketability".

By the end of the day the entire subject of my book had changed. The title had morphed into "Pink-slipped at 55". By end of the second day it became "Fired at Fifty". I also had the back cover finished. My book was taking shape, I had all my chapters captioned and outlined. I knew exactly where I was going. All I needed to do was to sit down and write. Anyone can take Julie's "Inspire A Book" workshop and come out at the end of the two days with an entire outline for a book, even if they never considered themselves a writer. The process really inspires people to consider how their life experience and knowledge could impact other people and help them on their journey.

On the second day of the workshop we discussed our target market. Well, I already knew my target market was 60% male and 40% female. I knew this from my online analytics with my social media with LinkedIn being the key platform. When I said this to the group, Julie asked, "Why do you think that is?" Then one of the other class members piped up with, "The men see you as being a safe hot." My head turned so fast, it almost popped off: and I didn't know what "safe hot" meant.

She explained to me that a "safe hot" was someone who was a bit of eye candy: smart and easy to talk to. Men felt they could talk, ask questions, and get coaching without having to worry about being hit on. They could have an enjoyable, friendly exchange without any worries of other strings attached.

This was a shock to my system because I had never thought of myself as being in that category! Me … eye candy? Wow. After years of thinking myself as plain, you can imagine what a shock this was to me. I felt kind of chuffed to tell the truth. You know, for once I felt really pleased about myself. I guess we just see the flaws in ourselves: not the beauty that others see.

What about you? Do you have knowledge and experience you could share in a book? Who is following you on your social media and do you know why they appreciate your unique experience? Do you know who your target market is? If not, give me a call. I can help you figure it out.

I just want to help people in any way I can. My motto is if it's legal, ethical, morally right, and non-fattening - I'll do it. My heart went out to all those grey-haired men and women sitting around networking tables. I could see most of them were just like me and looking for more clients. I also realized these people were mostly solopreneurs and couldn't afford my services for lead generation. I concluded that this wasn't my target market at all. Still, I wondered, what I could do to help all these people?

In November 2011 (as I mentioned earlier) I realized that I was using LinkedIn to get clients to teach them how to use LinkedIn to get their own clients. Why couldn't I teach all these people in my networking groups how to do the same? The big challenge was then to inspire them with my idea. I had to find out what people were willing to pay for my workshops. Was I getting my point across? For my first workshop I charged $20 per person if they registered in advance. I made a few bucks to cover my gas and minor expenses.

The facts from my first workshop:

12 people attended.

Two people attended for free.

One person, who attended for free, helped with recruiting and selling the workshop. He brought four people. The other person helped with registration.

I brought five people.

I paid the person helping me 20% of all the total registration dues for his help.

My gross sales were $128.00.

I was pleased with this outcome because it showed people were willing to pay $20 for a two-hour workshop. For the future I knew I had to find a better venue - hopefully free and I needed to charge a larger fee. Later, two gentlemen approached me with the idea of using their boardroom for a full day workshop and I jumped at the opportunity. We discussed an early bird rate of $147 and after a certain date the price increased to $197. I agreed to pay them $50 for each person they brought to the event.

When it came to the day of the workshop I had booked a videographer to build my on-line video training program for my new website. That alone was $500 and much more for all the editing. The room was free, or so I thought, but I was informed on the day of the workshop that it was going to cost $300. That was a bit of a surprise; however, I have yet to receive an invoice. Four people came. Three paid $147 and one was brought by one of the sponsors of the boardroom. He said he would waive his $50 if I would let the person come for $100. My gross profit on that event; (providing there still isn't an invoice) came to $541.

At that rate, I was definitely going to starve if I didn't have help from my husband. I was getting into debt at an alarming rate: and I was just getting started.

Since that time I have held three sessions of workshops. The first two I tried to market were cancelled due to a lack of registration, but since then I have started to figure out how to fill the seats. I have been sending messages through my social media networks and inviting people, but I seem to get a lot of people saying that they would like to attend who never do. At other events they hand me their business card and ask me to send them the link, but they don't sign up. I believe I'm not the only one who is having challenges getting people to register for workshops. It has a lot to do with the economy and the competitive field of social media education. The reports I have received from some of my cohorts in social media is that it takes a lot of hard work to get "butts in the seats". Nothing comes easy in this life. It all takes "elbow grease". We need to think of it as a process and simply keep on keeping on.

I have also offered 30-minute LinkedIn sessions to show people the five keys to get their LinkedIn running. These sessions cost $20 each. They are just a sampler and explain what they need to do. If they want the full on lesson, they need to either have a coaching session with me or come to my workshops. Today I'm using these 30 minute sessions to up sell my coaching and workshops. Now I am getting the picture of how to make my LinkedIn workshops and coaching sessions to work together. All I've needed to do is tweak it a little.

What can you do to help people? What is your strength in this area?

When Mr. No fired me I felt unwanted, rejected, unloved, and insignificant. I felt that nobody wanted me. Now, my life has come to the point where people are asking for my help. I get requests from people asking for my help to market their products and services. I'm receiving new clients at the rate of two per month and they pay me $1,000 a month to do lead generation for them. I now have the privilege of being able to sit back to assess the situation. It has been a blessing indeed.

As far as being wanted, this is a work in progress. I have been learning how to create value and urgency with my LinkedIn lead generation and workshops. As I'm writing this, I have a workshop coming up at the end of this month and people have already registered and paid for it. This is a work in progress. I just need to be persistent. I have discovered that people really do want to take my LinkedIn workshops; however, the economy is such that people really don't have the money to pay for training.

Earlier, I mentioned how my analytics state I have mostly male followers both on Twitter and LinkedIn. However, on Facebook, my followers are 60% female. Can you see why you need to be on all the key platforms? If I weren't on Facebook, I would have a diminished chance of ever reaching the female sector of the market.

I found Trilby Jeeves on LinkedIn. Her posts about her buffoonery workshops caught my eye. I was intrigued, so I invited her to be my guest on The Marketing Mentress show. What a treat it was to interview her. Trilby does not know this, but through her story, she has helped me with my public speaking. Trilby Jeeves shares her story with us.

Thank you, Trilby.

Finding Your Gorilla
by Trilby Jeeves

Years ago, long before I was even close to fifty, I was listening to Vicki Gabereau on the CBC. She was interviewing a career transition counselor. Vickie asked her guest, "Have you ever failed at being able to help someone?"

The counselor responded not really, although one

time she came close. Her client had been coming for a few sessions surmised they weren't able to find her "thing" and she was okay with it as her expectations were low. Her client then stood up and left the office.

The counselor was begrudgingly accepting her defeat when she spotted a book her client had left. She ran down the hall waving her book, "You forgot this!" Her client thanked her, but before they parted the counselor asked what her book was about. "Gorillas. I just love gorillas!" The counselor firmly stated, "Come back to my office."

You have probably guessed the end of this story. Through some digging, some creative thinking, and homework at the zoo, that client ended up with her dream job working with gorillas and never looked back.

The lesson is obvious and to me, inspiring. Her story served me well when I was going through my own transitions.

Ten years ago I was working as a costume set supervisor on a film set. I did this part time to support my acting career. Well, I fell on location and this fall sent me on a year of chiropractic treatments, which culminated into a massive herniated disc.

On April 10, 2003 I was crying in pain as I was driving to work: my right leg and foot gave out. Two days later, they were operating to get the herniation off of my sciatic nerve.

My postoperative journey then began. After many months of physiotherapy, my cat of 17 years was dying and the relationship I was in was ending. Soon after I found myself with a cane and a brace surrounded by a pile of boxes in a bachelor apartment wondering what now?

Well, when in doubt go to Paris. I visited my friend for three weeks and embraced my deficits (as the neurologist coldly called my remaining drop foot) and weaknesses with as much pizzazz as possible.

The change of scenery was good for me; however, when I returned I had to face a new phase. My disability insurance had long run out and I needed to do something. Years ago a government program enabled me to learn French; therefore, the Employment Insurance office (EI) might be able to offer some guidance. A counselor assessed me and suggested that I might be suitable for a small business course and suggested I apply if I had a business idea.

Small business, well, I grew up in a small business setting as my parents were artisans (weaving, pottery, and painting) and had their own shop. I knew it was tough. The fact was, I just wanted a job. That didn't happen so I came up with a couple of businesses. I had made and sold hats years ago so I wasn't completely foreign to the idea of producing something to sell. Years before, I had created a heated fleece scarf for actors to keep warm on cold film sets.

I pitched the idea to the EI business course and eventually I got into the nine-month program. There began my learning: logos, business plans, business cards, tag lines, financial projections, and everything you can think of to launch a small business. During that time I was sewing up a storm, attending craft fairs, recruiting friends to fold scarves, selling, and finally taking the step of hiring a manufacturer.

Sometimes during the course I would burst into tears when I had to give a progress presentation about my progress. I'm sure everyone rolled their eyes and thought what an actress. Well, they weren't that far off the mark. I wasn't following my true self and my deeper passions. I had convinced myself that my scarves would take off and support my art. It was a fallacy. As much as I liked them, I didn't love them and the business was already taking up all of my time.

It wasn't easy to change course and I continued to plod on so I could prove to everyone I could succeed.

Finally, after a couple of years later, I knew I had to stop. Just stop.

"To unpathed waters, undreamed shores."
William Shakespeare

It was in the shower one morning when I was reminded of my love to perform and of a very rich moment in my acting past when Le Bouffon (a unique way of acting in an extreme way) woke up my world. Suddenly, a strong vision appeared and I chose to acknowledge it. I felt a rush of adrenalin and as I reached for my towel in an urgent manner. I needed to write this down. Now.

A workshop! A "Buffoonery" workshop for actors so they could find freedom in their performances. I was excited. I locked the door, put on some music, and designed for two weeks straight. I envisioned how to get people to find their bouffons and apply it to texts (monologues and scenes) in a two-day workshop. I hardly noticed the two weeks pass by.

I made a poster, contacted friends, and advertised to the best of my ability: five people signed up.

Those five people had a blast. They learned, I learned and they told their friends.

I did another workshop. More people showed up. Even non-actors. Well, almost six years later and approximately 800 bouffons later (at various levels) I still love, developing, and expanding my Buffoonery Workshop.

The last six years I have been on an apprenticeship of marketing, networking, defining and re-defining what I do. It's been exciting: personal growth; going into social media kicking and screaming until I realized it was actually fun and effective; being frustrated when I had to cancel a workshop; being deliriously happy and rewarded watching significant breakthroughs; tons of laughter; and travelling far to teach.

I remember attending a structured Business Networking International (BNI) breakfast as someone's guest in my early buffoonery days. I dressed for success and gave my 60-second elevator speech to the group.

"I give buffoonery workshops." This always created a bit of a stir as I wasn't exactly in a typical category. Relieved it was over, I sat down and poured myself some water. Ice cubes came tumbling out onto the white linen covered table giving me a little more than my allotted 60 seconds of attention. I looked at everyone staring. "Well… I'm in buffoonery!" Everyone laughed. Whew. I even got invited for a one on one coffee directly after with one of the members. Apparently that world needed a bouffon!

Today, my growth continues and as I write my story I wonder what you might get from it. Never give up? Learn some structure from one source and apply it to one you love? Find what you love and figure out how you can earn a living from it? I don't think I ever thought that I would earn my living from buffoonery.

One thing I truly realized and I knew it in my head, but now I know it in my heart, loving what you do, what ever the reason, what ever the vocation, is good for your soul, your heart, your health, your family, and most importantly, you.

I like to remember the advice flight attendants give during the safety demonstrations, "If the oxygen masks drop down, make sure you put yours on first before helping anyone else."

When you are you, you can be there in an inspiring way for others. And, if you are doing something you don't like, is there a way to change things so that you do like?

Here's to hoping you find your bouffon or gorilla. And, don't forget your sense of humour along the way.

My top Trilby suggestions as a result of my ongoing journey.

1-Trust your gut. It can really guide you to make the correct decisions.

2-Take 10-15 minute naps, and pay attention to images, ideas that come to you as you're drifting. These times have been super helpful to me. Your muse will love you and it's a great excuse to lie down.

3- If you take yourself too seriously it will be harder to take the knocks, and leap over the obstacles, laugh at those ice cube moments!

4- Be careful who and what you listen to when asking for advice. Review tip number one.

5- Read a lot of business books, go to short seminars, and review tip number one again.

6- Consider getting a business coach, or a life coach even if it's for a short time. He or she can guide you to some good habits or to your true calling. I hired a business coach. It helps.

7- Network, even if you're just looking for a job, opportunities can arise from all kinds of interesting sources.

8- Help other people. Helping someone else can actually remind you of your attributes, especially if you're getting too self-critical.

9- If you are looking for a job, or want to be an entrepreneur, use all the social media tools. They're great for promotions and connecting. LinkedIn is especially good for job search.

10- Finally, be grateful for what you have. I started writing a daily gratitude journal a couple of years ago and it has helped me so much. I write down a few things I'm grateful for from every day and I post it on Facebook and Twitter. That ritual helps me to keep doing it, I am surprised by the feedback I get and how many people followed suit. It's a healthy movement that can help you through the tough days and make the good days even sweeter.

Thank you Trilby.

Trilby Jeeves

www.buffooneryworkshops.com
www.trilbyjeeves.com
Amazing. And Kucki Low's, "This is Kucki Your Pilot Speaking," her story is about her life and how she became the first woman pilot in South Africa. What an amazing story. I met Kucki at a workshop we attended together. When she shared her story with me, I just had to have her on my show.

I asked Kucki to contribute to my book so my readers could understand how you can achieve anything in your life if you put your mind to it. Here is her contribution.

Thank you, Kucki.

This Is Kucki Your Pilot Speaking
Fasten your seat belts! We are going to have some fun.

When facing challenging times "fun" and "joy" are considered as unnecessary or even frivolous emotions. Yet, those are exactly the emotions that will often open up opportunities and connect us with the right people who can take us to the next step. You can probably remember a time when you were really happy, enjoying life and bingo – you got a great idea.

It's amazing where our lives can take us, if we are determined to follow our passion regardless of obstacles. I should know because I certainly had a few.

Due to a combination of passion and circumstances, I was fortunate to achieve my goal of becoming the first female airline pilot and the first female flight instructor in South Africa. This was back in the 1970's. Looking back, and considering my circumstances at the time, I was probably the most unlikely candidate to achieve those landmarks.

Forty years ago flying was certainly a very male dominated environment. To put it into perspective, even today the number of female airline pilots is only around three percent worldwide; which I believe you will agree is a rather small percentage. I was a petit woman in a man's world. Nothing about me screamed pilot. Although it was exciting to be a pioneer, I had to overcome my own fears and challenges. I had to be willing to get out of my comfort zone to step onto a new path.

Through circumstances beyond my control, I had to leave school when I was fifteen years old. This meant that I didn't have the required maths or science credits. Plus, English wasn't my first language, although I did have some German. Those facts certainly presented a big challenge for me when I had to write the exam for my commercial license - which I failed hopelessly the first time.

At that point I had to make a choice. I could buy into my family and friends well-meaning belief systems as to what was possible for me. Or, I could trust that I had the ability to achieve my dream. It was just going to take a lot more determination and hard work than I had bargained for. This belief has served me well throughout my life.

What has gotten me through my challenges is my passion and determination to achieve my dream no matter what. Actually, that could be said for anything any of us want to do in life. I also attribute my success to the great mentors in my life: Mentors who believed in my ability to achieve my dreams when I was still a little shaky in that department and were willing to help me. We all need people who believe and encourage us to go after our dreams.

There is a quote by Tom Robbins that says: "It's never too late to have a happy childhood."

I love that quote. I think it speaks to the fact that it's not what life presents to us, it's how we interpret it and what we do with it that makes the difference. It always amazes me how many people still blame their parents or events in their childhood for not achieving their dreams and living the life they would really love to live. There is such over whelming evidence of people who succeeded in spite of huge obstacles in their early life. It's those stories that often inspire us to dig deeper and find the courage to succeed - no matter what.

My childhood wasn't conventional by any definition. I was born in Austria and I didn't live with my parents for the first six years of my life. In 1953 my parents emigrated to what was then South West Africa, now called Namibia.

I spent most of my school years in various boarding schools feeling lonely and lost. As a teenager, just as I was reconnecting with my parents, they both died within two years of each other. We owned a photography business and whenever I was home I loved watching my father take portraits. I was eager to learn all I could about photography from him. It was also an opportunity for me to spend time with him and for us to get a little closer.

When I was 15 my father had his first heart attack and was unable to continue working. My parents decided their only option was to take me out of school to run our photography business: with my father guiding me from his bedside. Even though I was only 15, with my father's guidance and my parents putting all their trust in me, I rose to the challenge and that changed everything for me.

That was such a happy period in my life. At last I got to be with parents. I felt loved and appreciated by the two people I adored and admired. Unconsciously instead of expecting to receive love, I had given what I most wanted and it had boomeranged back to me. Looking back that was a good lesson for me to learn early on; unfortunately, that period was short lived

I was seventeen years old when my mother committed suicide. Almost two years later my father had his second heart attack and passed away. I was nineteen and alone.

We are fortunate if we have had a secure and happy childhood; however, our challenges also become our greatest teachers and leave us with some valuable gifts. Succeeding at running our photography business at such an early age gave me confidence: I could do anything I set my mind to. That was probably one of the biggest gifts my parents gave me.

Although losing my parents at such an early age was traumatic, I wouldn't have missed the four years I spent with them (prior to their death) for anything, not even for an education. It was a pivotal point for me. I believe that experience set the tone for the rest of my life.

There was nothing in my life experiences that would have predicted where my life would take me and what I would achieve. I didn't land in my crib with a passion for flying. I am often asked in an interview: "Did you always want to fly?"

My answer: "No, it was never on my radar as a possibility. I had never considered flying as a possible career."

I stumbled onto flying by chance. I had the opportunity to do some aerial photography and when I experienced the thrill of flying for the first time: I was hooked. It was the most exhilarating feeling for me. I loved every minute of it. My joy meter has always been my most reliable indicator. I just knew I wanted to fly: and fly I did.

Even though many years have passed since I left my flying career behind, my excitement for life and for following my passion hasn't changed. I think very few people are born with a burning passion for something; for example, a pianist or dancer.

For most of us; however, that is not the case. Generally we have more than one passion. We can be passionate about different things at different stages of our lives. It's what we do with that passion that determines the degree of fulfillment and happiness we feel in our lives.

For me, in my twenties, I was passionate about flying. In my thirties I was equally, if not more excited about being a wife and mother. Creating a loving and harmonious home in which to raise our son was something that I felt I had missed out on as a child: Don't we all want to provide our children with the things we feel we didn't have?

In my forties I ventured into business and I started a number of enterprises of my own. They were great challenges for me and were driving forces in my life at that time.

Seven years ago I discovered Kundalini Yoga and meditation. They have become a total passion for me and now I have shifted my attention towards a more inward journey.

Today I'm in my sixties. I feel so fortunate to be able to completely re-invent myself and go on this amazing journey of being an author and speaker. Inspiring others to live up to their full potential and follow their passion excites me as much as anything that I have done so far.

A new passion can show up at any stage of our life, or sometimes we're forced through circumstances to re-evaluate what is important and what we're really fervent about. When life throws us a curve ball, instead of seeing it as a negative why not consider it a gift? The gift of discovering we can make a great living doing something we really love and perhaps we wouldn't have discovered that gift if we weren't forced to shift gears.

Think back to a time when something really excited you and gave you that feeling of joy. What did you do with that thought? Did you follow that trail? Or did you dismiss it by saying: "I don't think I could do that, not at this stage."

Be alert to that little voice in the back of your mind. That's normally when the logical mind kicks in and gives us all the reasons why we couldn't possibly do that; for example: We don't have the education; we are too old; we don't have the financial resources or whatever the reasons might be, for not following through on that passion. Maybe now is the time to stifle that voice.

If I had listened to my little voice and not followed my passion I would have missed out on so many fabulous experiences along the way. For me, passion, enthusiasm, and a trust in things always working out are essential for living a fulfilled and happy life - no matter what age. Being excited about life is what keeps you young. I'm probably more excited about what lies ahead for me now than I have ever been.

Often people feel as we get older our life becomes less exciting. I think the exact opposite. One advantage of being older (and there certainly are many) is that you are more comfortable with yourself. You are more confident and you don't give a rip what anybody thinks about you. That is a luxury that comes with age.

I think we really owe it to ourselves to live our passion and do something that really excites us, because if we are happy and love what we do, we light up the world around us and inspire others to follow their passion.

Being passionate about life and anticipating good things to show up is what makes us want to jump out of bed in the morning. If you're not quite certain what your passion is yet, just follow the trail of what gives you joy. It will take you towards your passion.

And the next time that you see something and think: "Wow, wouldn't it be great if I could do that" and if you hear that little voice in the back of your head saying: "I don't think I could do that." I hope that my determination to live joyously and follow my passion, in spite of some difficult circumstances, will have activated the thought within you if she can do it, so can I.

Kucki Low
www.kuckilow.com

I just love Kucki's insight and there are other wonderful authors who I have had the honour of interviewing on my show. As you can see, the evolution of my podcasting career has been richer than I ever could have imagined. Below is a list of other books you may enjoy reading.

- Robin J. Elliott – "Joint Ventures for Life"
- Diane Stringam Tolley – "Carving Angels" and "Kris Kringle's Magic"
- Doug Dickerson – "Leaders Without Borders: 9 Essentials for Everyday Leaders"
- Angela Crocker – "Creating a Social Network"
- Manon Boliger – "What Patients Don't say If Doctors Don't Ask"
- Michael Losier – "Law of Attraction"
- Neil Godin – "Selling in the (Comfort) Zone"
- Phil Taylor – "Set Yourself on Fire"
- Roy Osing – "Be Different Or Be Dead: Your Business Survival Guide"
- Roy Prevost – "Turbocharge Your Retail Business"

As this book is now coming to an end I would like to wrap up with a couple of points. As I've stated social media and mobile marketing have changed how we do business today.

The second point is about the boomer generation born between 1945 and 1965. Eight point two million babies were born in Canada during this period (Vital Statistics Canada Census 2011). In a few short years, 25% of the population will be over 65 years of age. Statistics reveal that the younger generations won't be able to cover the costs of Canada pensions and old age security, let alone any top-up programs for the boomers.

Here is another statistic for you. Over 70% of the boomer generation isn't financially prepared for their retirement and they're depending on the government plans to see them through. The first wave of boomers hit 65 in 2010. Can you see what is about to happen in the next 20 years?

There is a huge new economy growing and developing with the boomers. They are healthier than previous generations; thus, they are living longer. They have great mental acuity and physical capabilities. Boomers are the most highly educated group ever in history. (You don't have to go far to find that there were more boomers who completed secondary education with a profession than any generation before them. Check out Statistics Canada – Education Indicators in Canada 2010) So, when they are "Fired at Fifty" they are still very capable.

I see this every time I attend a networking meeting, or check out who is following me in my social media. Most of my followers are over 45 years of age. LinkedIn has an average user age of 43 years old; that means that there are a lot of people on LinkedIn who are over 50. The boomers will live longer and work longer than any previous generation. (Research is showing that obesity is predicted to be a huge challenge with the younger generations, causing many health challenges. Statistics Canada – Life Expectancy by Birth by Sex and by Province and Statistics Canada – Microsimulation – Health Models) It will be more common to see the boomers working well into their 70s and even into their 80s. And, it is becoming more common to see the boomer generation creating their own businesses at this point in their lives. When you attend business trade shows and check out the tables present, what do you see? From what I have witnessed, the average age of the people running those booths is 50.

Boomers are starting network marketing businesses when they don't have the funds to start a conventional business. The boomers are buying franchises, so they can shortcut the learning phase and simply follow a pattern as a means to start making money sooner. Why do you think that boomers are starting their own businesses? It isn't because they are bored. It is because they can't find gainful employment that will pay them enough to cover living expenses and savings for their retirement. If they want to get ahead, as I see it, the only option boomers have today is to own their own business.

A report from the Vancouver Sun newspaper by Julian Beltrame (September 29, 2012) states that over half-million people in Canada have recently started their own businesses. He also states that, "Older Canadians are more likely to start their own firms … the over 50 crowd represents 30% of all the new start-ups." Beltrame reports "The number of individuals starting businesses in the educational services field has risen by 65% since 2007, the fastest growth of any, followed by a 20 per cent increase in health care. B.C. leads with start-ups representing 39% of the employed population."

A large factor allowing Canadians and people around the world to start their own businesses is the new media. People can start their own businesses without a lot of overhead, because they can work from home. This is also referred to as cocooning.

These boomers are hungry for this knowledge of how to use the new media. They are catching up to their kids. Take my family, it might have been my son who dragged me into the new media and the computer age kicking and screaming, but if the truth be known: today I know more about the new media than all my children combined.

My forefathers came to this land to escape poverty and oppression (serfdom) only to end up back in serfdom again. Serfdom meaning working in jobs for a wage that dictates to us the type of home we live in, the clothes we wear, our entire lifestyle.

The business owners of today are fed up with this type of bondage and control. Owning your own business is the only way to combat serfdom through jobs and government taxation. Owning our own businesses is the new direction of empowerment. It is what our ancestors craved when they first settled in this country. Isn't it interesting how we have come full circle?

Writing this book has been therapeutic. It's both exhilarating and rejuvenating. It has also helped me to get my life in proper perspective. I would never have thought in a million years that I would be writing my book until I met Julie: she has been an inspiration to me. I believe everyone has a book in them. Start writing your book today and even if you don't end up publishing it, it will give you a new prospective on your situation.

Julie has a gift for editing and she coaches us through the process of writing our books. I have learned the importance of presenting yourself as professionally as possible and that the book can lead to so many opportunities because of the credibility that comes with being a published author. You can use your book as a platform for your business to help with getting media engagements or speaking at a seminar. It's a strategic marketing strategy to promote your business. Harv T Eker, considered one of the world's marketing leaders, talks about the book being your "100 page business card" and that every entrepreneur should have a book as a marketing tool.

My final question to you is, "Are you going to ride the wave of these tsunamis, or are you going to be left in their wake?" I wish all of my readers all the best on their journey… now, go make your dreams come true.

Author Biography

 This vivacious, enthusiastic and intelligent entrepreneur, Christine Till, has 20+ years of marketing background in the hospitality industry, senior care industry and business management profession. She brings to your modern business theatre a wealth of knowledge, experience and expertise in marketing. She is known for her unique relationship marketing approach through internet radio, commonly known as podcasting. The gift of a podcast is always remembered because it feels so good to be listened to and have an opportunity to speak about yourself and what you do.

Being a person of integrity, always true to her word, is of utmost importance to Christine and she admires others who also practice integrity in the way they do business, as well.

Christine specializes in LinkedIn and public speaking, teaching people how to use LinkedIn to build lasting relationships with their clients.

She teaches how to use LinkedIn to build connections with key people for your business. Looking for people who want to be different in their business.

Her goal is to help small businesses find their unique position in the marketplace through the use of LinkedIn. Target market is the 50+ who suddenly find themselves with a pink slip, 5-15 years before they are ready to retire.

Christine's book, Fired at Fifty, is a story of her journey written in a self-help fashion, to help others who have found themselves in the same position...out of work with no prospects.

To find out more about the services offered by Christine Till:

The Marketing Mentress
Social media coaching and Linked In workshops from beginners to experts:

- Linked in 101 – Creating a stellar LinkedIn profile that performs
- Linked In 201 – Connecting without being connected; the secrets of the groups;   targeting your specific market.
- Linked in 301 – Getting recommendations without asking for them; build your   personal marketing plan with your social media; building your credibility through LinkedIn.

Having challenges with figuring out how to use your LinkedIn and other social media? Receive Personal one-on-one coaching: done in person or over Skype. Create your own personal marketing system with LinkedIn. Learn how to manage all your social media together from one platform.

Websites:
www.marketingmentress.podbean.com
www.practicalpodcasting.com

Email: christine@practicalpodcasting.com

Tel no.: 604-945-1000

Interviews:
Book media interviews through Christine Till at the above contact information, or through Influence Publishing:
info@influencepublishing.com

Find me on social media at:

- Twitter: @mktgmentress
- Facebook: www.facebook.com/TheMarketingMentress
- LinkedIn: www.ca.linkedin.com/in/christinetill/
- Email: christine@practicalpodcasting.com

If you want to get on the path to be a published author by **Influence Publishing** please go to **www.InspireABook.com**

Inspiring books that influence change

More information on our other titles and how to submit your own proposal can be found at **www.InfluencePublishing.com**

CPSIA information can be obtained at www.ICGtesting.com
Printed in the USA
LVOW05s0357220314

378442LV00010B/51/P